get your sparkle on

get your sparkle on

Create and wear the gems that make you shine

by **Lindsay Cain** with **Sarah B. Weir**

Photographs by **Ellen McDermott**
Illustrations by **Rachel Stone**

CHRONICLE BOOKS

SAN FRANCISCO

Text copyright © 2006 by Lindsay Cain and Sarah B. Weir.

Photographs copyright © 2006 by Ellen McDermott.

Illustrations copyright © 2006 by Rachel Stone.

Photo credits: page 27 courtesy of Corbis; page 42 copyright © Priscilla Rattazzi; page 62 courtesy of Corbis; page 75 copyright © The Imogen Cunningham Trust; page 110 copyright © Amanda Havey.

Library of Congress Cataloging-in-Publication Data:

Cain, Lindsay.

Get your sparkle on: create and wear the gems that make you shine / by Lindsay Cain with Sarah Weir.

p. cm.

ISBN-10: 0-8118-5240-7

ISBN-13: 978-0-8118-5240-1

1. Jewelry making–Amateurs' manual. I. Weir, Sarah. II. Title.

TT212.C32 2006

745.594'2—dc22

2005029178

Manufactured in China

Designed by **SUGAR**

Distributed in Canada by Raincoast Books
9050 Shaughnessy Street
Vancouver, British Columbia V6P 6E5

10 9 8 7 6 5 4 3 2 1

Chronicle Books LLC
85 Second Street
San Francisco, California 94105
www.chroniclebooks.com

Dedicated to Tyler, my most precious gem.

This book was a whirlwind project, and many people worked extra hard on often crazy deadlines to make it happen. Sincere and special thanks go to Ellen McDermott; Rachel Stone; Nina Collins; Jodi Davis; Renata Chaplynsky; Teril Turner; Jen Weinberg; Muffy Nixon; Mason Rather; Ali Nichols; Annette Rose-Shapiro; Nordin Merchant; Jared Grossman; Dora Grossman-Weir; Jennifer Sims; Jen Kripas; my amazing staff in New York, Chicago, and Greenwich; and Sarah Weir, my outstanding partner without whom *Sparkle* would not have been realized.

table of contents

THE BASICS

9 • **INTRODUCTION**

12 • **ROCK OF AGES**

16 • **CHARM SCHOOL FUNDAMENTALS**
   16   Tool Box for Your Jewel Box

21 • **BASIC NECKLACE ASSEMBLY**
   21   Stringing
   22   Adding a Clasp:
        The Crimp-Flattening Method
   23   Adding a Clasp:
        The Fold-Over Crimping Method
   24   Wire-Wrapping Technique

GEMSTYLES & PROJECTS

27 • **CLASSIC GEMSTYLE**
28 Not-Your-Grandmother's Pearl Necklace
30 Girly Pearl Necklace

35 • **PREPPY GEMSTYLE**
36 Think Pink … and Green Necklace
38 All-Tied-Up Ribbon Cuff
40 Ribbon Belt

42 • **ULTRA-CHIC GEMSTYLE**
43 The Ultimate Accessory Necklace
47 Peek Inside: Ali's Jewel Box
48 Chain, Chain, Chain Earrings

51 • **BRIDAL GEMSTYLE**
52 It's-My-Party Teardrop Necklace
54 Bejeweled Bridesmaid Party
58 Stemgems Wineglass Markers
60 Wedding Jewels

62 • **PARTY GIRL GEMSTYLE**
64 Kicky Knickers
66 Extreme Makeover Earrings
68 Peek Inside: Lindsay's Jewel Box

69 • **SMARTY-PANTS GEMSTYLE**
70 Sassy Glasses
72 Back-to-School Charm Bracelet

77 • **BOHEMIAN GEMSTYLE**
78 Chunky Monkey Choker
80 Knock-on-Wood Bracelet
82 Bewitched, Bothered, and Bejeweled
84 Birthstones

86 • **EXECUTIVE GEMSTYLE**
88 Rock, Scissors, Paperweight
90 Odd-Bead-Out Necklace
92 Peek Inside: Teri's Jewel Box

93 • **BEACH BABE GEMSTYLE**
94 She Sells Seashells Necklace
98 Two-of-a-Kind Anklets
100 Catch-a-Wave Choker

102 • **ROCK STAR GEMSTYLE**
104 Flea Market Makeover Jewels
106 Shoulder-Duster Earrings

111 • **PARK AVENUE GEMSTYLE**
112 French Knot Necklace
114 Razzle-Dazzle Tassel Earrings

FINISHING TOUCHES

118 Garage Sale Necklace
119 Resources

PART ONE

THE BASICS

introduction

One chilly morning when I was in first grade, my mother wrapped a bright orange fur muffler around my neck and, ignoring my whining protests, scooted me out the door to the school bus. "You all wear the same uniform—don't be afraid to be different, Lindsay!" she hollered and waved as the bus door slammed shut. That was a tough ride to school. But what I didn't realize at the time was that she was showing me how to use style and accessories as a way to stand out from the crowd.

My mom's closet housed a refrigerator-sized safe brimming with amazing treasures. No, it wasn't filled with trays of rare diamonds and priceless emeralds. Instead, there were boxes of vintage costume collectibles, jewels from famed American craftsmen, and a bear claw necklace that scared me to death. There were ropes and ropes of glittering stones, and carved metal beads rolled into soft, colorful fabrics from all over the world. And would you believe it? Not a pearl in sight. No, my mother did *not* wear pearls. Instead, she sought out the unusual, the funky, the gorgeous. Her style showed that she definitely wasn't afraid to be different. Now, fast-forward twenty years: my sparkle may not be exactly like my mother's, but she certainly taught me how to find my own.

The goal of *Get Your Sparkle On* is to help you create jewelry that will make you shine and stand out from the crowd. Until recently, brilliant clusters of honey citrines or multistrand torsades of aquamarine nuggets were seen only paired with the Chanel jackets on ladies who lunch or gracing the cleavage of Hollywood divas. But now, these gems can be worn by anyone who wants to make a bold fashion statement and express her love for jewelry. Nobody loves jewelry as fervently as Elizabeth Taylor, who, in her over-the-top homage, *Elizabeth Taylor: My Love Affair with Jewelry*, describes how she wheedled one of her favorite pieces, an exquisite diamond and crystal lily-of-the-valley brooch, out of Rex Harrison. "You're the stingiest man alive," she chided Harrison, "your giving me this pin would be doubly important because it would signify a personal triumph over your naturally stingy nature." Of course, not many gals can accessorize (or cajole) with Liz Taylor's signature sass and aplomb. Yet today's gemstone jewelry offers a playful, sexy, elegant, and *affordable* way to add some sparkle to your wardrobe—especially if you make it yourself. Whether you favor big, swinging chandelier earrings or a flirty trio of layered necklaces, jewelry is the ultimate expression of femininity and personal style.

Get Your Sparkle On features projects that are simple to make. First, you will learn a few basic jewelry-making techniques, and then you will put your newfound skills to work making gorgeous necklaces, earrings, bracelets, and more! Each project features easy step-by-step directions and bright, yummy photographs showing the finished piece. To make the book easy to navigate, and to inspire innovative ways to wear your foxy new bijoux, I've grouped the projects by their "gemstyles." So if one day you find yourself channeling Joan Jett, flip to the chapter entitled "Rock Star Gemstyle." If the next day you are feeling more Jackie O., check out the chapter on "Park Avenue Gemstyle." You get the idea.

Get Your Sparkle On speaks to all of your style whims. But it doesn't stop there. *Get Your Sparkle On* also offers loads of tips on how to make over your buried treasures and finally do something wonderful with all those bits and bobs rattling around in the bottom of your jewel box. Maybe you adore that vintage coral brooch but can't imagine where to pin it. Perhaps Granny's hand-me-down chunky amethyst bracelet is so lovely…but so 1962. Or perchance your heart thumps "Barneys" but your pocketbook responds "Claire's." This book will teach you how to create your own gorgeous jewelry (*Bye-bye*, Barneys.), make over peculiar or priceless old pieces (*Hello*, Granny!), and discover your own gemstyle!

With lots of how-to projects, accessorizing ideas, and fun and informative sidebars, *Get Your Sparkle On* demonstrates how you, too, can choose, create, and don the baubles that will make you look like a million bucks—*without* breaking the bank. Now you're ready to rock.

twinkle, twinkle, little you.

femmegems

After slogging through the nine-to-five routine for a few years after college, I was abruptly awakened to my true calling when the owner of a chic Easthampton boutique nearly ripped the homemade necklace from my throat, shouting, "Where did you get this? I need it in my store!" Soon after, armed only with a spool of .014-gauge silver wire and a sack full of colorful rocks, I quit my day job to start producing jewelry full-time. A few years and hundreds of Diet Cokes later, I decided to enter an accessories trade show at the Jacob Javits Center in New York City. By the end of the third day, my jewelry line had been picked up by twenty stores. And, four seasons later, the number of retailers topped seventy. Diamonds may be a girl's best friend, but I had decided to hedge my bets on jade, smoky topaz, and rose quartz briolettes.

Although running a business out of my apartment had temporarily limited my social life to visits with my new best buddies at Kinko's, one afternoon a visit from an old friend sparked the inspiration that would lead me up a new path. Most designers stow their creations in shelved trays, but I prefer to keep mine where I can see them, so I had organized my work over an entire wall of hooks. When my friend spied the display, her eyes lit up as if she were a kid in a candy store. She dropped her handbag and began running her fingers through the strands of garnet, mother-of-pearl, and turquoise that bedecked my apartment walls. She twirled them together by the handful and got completely caught up in fantasizing about the pieces I could someday make for her... or that she could make for herself, with my help.

Instantly, I saw my future: a retail store where women, with some friendly guidance and the best raw materials, could tap into their creativity and make unique, gorgeous jewelry for themselves. It would take the lackluster bead-store concept to the next level—a chic, fun, and sexy venue stocked with beautiful and valuable materials and staffed by knowledgeable and helpful jewelry designers. With the help of my then-boyfriend (now my husband) and a few months of hard work, I opened Femmegems, a luxurious do-it-yourself jewelry-making boutique in New York City's hip NoLita neighborhood.

The neighborhood's trendy gals soon flocked to the shop and returned with their curious friends, colleagues, cousins, and grandmothers. It seemed that everyone wanted to make jewelry like the pieces they had coveted at Bergdorf's (at a fraction of the price). Soon after, I opened more of my little jewel boxes in new locations, including Greenwich, Connecticut, and at Henri Bendel and Marshall Field's flagship stores.

Our motto? "Awake the designer within!"

*rock of ages

What's the world's oldest profession? Nope. Not that. The right answer is more likely jewelry making. The history of gemstone jewelry stretches back as far as the history of humankind. Beads were one of the first manmade objects. They are found in nearly every archaeological site inhabited by early humans, who used them as currency and as amulets to ward off sickness and danger. It wasn't long before we learned how to drill pearls, quartz, and other gems and began wearing them mainly for their beauty.

The ancient Egyptians did much to advance metal working and lapidary techniques and adorned themselves with a variety of gemstones set into huge collars, diadems, cuffs, earrings, and rings. So intense was their love for jewels that the royals were buried with them (along with their mummified cats and slews of slaughtered servants), believing they could carry their possessions into the afterlife. The Phoenicians disseminated Egyptian techniques throughout the Mediterranean, where they reached the Greeks, who took craftsmanship to new heights and wrought exquisitely delicate, intricate jewelry. The Romans then inherited the Greek techniques and used them to fashion bold, striking pieces. They also imported new types of jewels from their colonies and trading partners—diamonds from India, sapphires from Sri Lanka, and amber and jet from the Baltic region.

By the Middle Ages in Europe, jewelry had become a clear indicator of status and wealth, which the upper-class leaders were determined to protect. Through the enactment of "sumptuary laws," various rulers and church officials tried to restrict the common folk from wearing gold or gemstones. (It's not surprising that it was the women who repeatedly challenged these dictates and won back their right to adorn themselves!) Seeing the importance of jewels as an economic commodity, Emperor Charlemagne put an end to the ancient custom of burial with jewelry, in order to keep the precious metals and gems in circulation among those who could afford them.

The size and elaborate style of bijoux from the time of the Renaissance on mirrored the bulging wealth of the European aristocracy. The elite wore twists of pearls through their hair; jewels on their bodices, hats, and belts; stacks of rings on their fingers; and enough layered medallions to make Missy Elliott look austere. Louis XIV demanded diamonds on everything from his doublet cloth to his buttons to the buckles on his high-heeled shoes. Flashy footwear did not begin with Manolo.

Although the middle classes couldn't afford such decadence, plenty of men, women, and children sported at least a pretty ring. In 1912, construction workers in London dug up a perfectly preserved cache of baubles, dubbed "the Cheapside Hoard," in what had been a jewelry shop for wealthy commoners during the mid-seventeenth century. There were fine rings set with both cabochons and faceted stones, and long links of gold chain decorated with dainty enamel flowers, amethysts, and pearls, which would have been sold by the foot. Since men of the era often wore one dandy earring, the collection contained fancy, tiered danglers in singles and pairs.

Jewelry-making techniques changed little for centuries, utilizing the finest materials and craftsmanship to produce beautiful works of art. With the advent of the Industrial Revolution came mass production, which became the primary method of creating jewelry quickly and inexpensively for a wide market. However, despite industrialization, various artisanal waves such as the Arts and Crafts Movement returned to ancient techniques to create fine and detailed jewels. Then, in the 1930s, fashion designers like Coco Chanel and Elsa Schiaparelli began whimsically mixing real rocks and fakes, changing the direction of the jewelry industry. Driven by both the public's hunger for the baubles worn by Hollywood glamour girls and bleak economic conditions, an enormous market for costume-couture jewelry emerged. Suddenly it was considered acceptable, even stylish, to wear knockoffs instead of their high-priced counterparts. And in the midst of the Great Depression, who could afford the real thing anyway?

Today, we are experiencing our own modern-day Renaissance in the appreciation of authentic jewels. Although fakes can be truly fabulous, there is nothing like a real gemstone, whose pure color and flashing fire were formed deep in our great Earth. Hollywood stars and royalty have never stopped wearing fine jewelry loaded with precious stones, but now new mining techniques and geological discoveries have made gemstone jewelry available to anyone with an eye for true beauty.

great moments in bling

BC

c. 2500
The ancient Egyptians spice up their white linen shifts with colored jewels, becoming the first culture to exploit the fashion potential of gemstone jewelry.

c. 35
According to legend, Marc Antony comments to Cleopatra that her banquet is not as sumptuously decadent as he hoped. "I'll show you decadent," snarls the Egyptian queen, who promptly quaffs a monster pearl dropped in a goblet of wine.

AD

529
Codex of Justinian enacts sumptuary laws restricting adornment with jewelry to the nobility. No fair!

c. 800
Emperor Charlemagne attempts to keep the wealth of jewelry in circulation by forbidding the ancient custom of burial with one's bling.

1415
In the famed Battle of Agincourt, a huge, irregularly shaped red spinel (misidentified as a ruby) mounted on Henry V's helmet saves the Black Prince from a fatal sword blow to the head.

1440
In an early example of why French women have all the fun, Agnes Sorel, mistress to Charles VII, becomes the first European commoner to wear diamonds.

c. 1600
Responding to an influx of fabulous fakes, the authorities in Venice decree the production of phony pearls to be punishable by the loss of the right hand.

1623
The invention of the faceted "rose cut" partially unlocks the fire of diamonds.

1748
The discovery of the ruins of Pompeii leads to a craze in neoclassical jewelry styles. A decade later, Halley's comet sparks shooting-star designs.

1785
A scandal surrounding Marie-Antoinette's supposed purchase without payment of a fabulously extravagant diamond necklace is one of the catalysts leading to the French Revolution.

1849
On a royal whim, Queen Victoria orders the huge, legendary, and coveted Koh-i-noor diamond to be recut. The results are less than brilliant.

1850
Diamonds are imported to the United States for the first time.

1857
The first Mardi Gras celebration takes place in New Orleans. The tradition of throwing necklaces into the crowd from colorful floats eventually evolves into one that blends merrymaking, jewelry, and appreciation of the female body. "Show me your. . . beads!"

1886
Tiffany's (founded 1837) develops their famous diamond setting, which shows off the stone's brilliance by elevating it on prongs. This setting remains the standard to this day.

1890

Shrouded in secrecy, Japanese scientist Mikimoto invents a commercial method of culturing pearls.

c. 1900

In a chic and clever meeting of sparkle and politics, suffragettes don jewelry featuring green, white, and violet gems, the initials of which stand for their battle cry, "Give women the vote!"

Fans rush to imitate thespian Sarah Bernhardt's divine Art Nouveau jewels—the first time a celebrity has exerted such an effect on fashion trends.

1907

The superintendent of the Premier Mine in South Africa digs the world's largest diamond, the Cullinan I, out of a pit with his penknife. The 3,106-carat raw stone (weighing 1.6 pounds) is split *very carefully* and cut down into a pear-shaped, 530.2-carat beauty to be presented to the British Crown.

c. 1920

Josephine Baker and her racy dance revue inspire a craze for African-style jewels.

1922

The luminous treasures discovered in King Tutankhamun's tomb spark a mania for ancient Egyptian revival jewels.

1930s

The costume jeweler Trifari begins to sell copies of Hollywood gems to the glamour-hungry masses.

1958

After a cursed history that included the bankruptcies, untimely deaths, and suicides of some of its owners, the fabulous deep-blue 67-carat Hope Diamond is donated by jeweler Harry Winston to the Smithsonian Institution.

1987

The jewelry collection of the late Duchess of Windsor Wallis Simpson is auctioned for a record-breaking 50 million dollars.

1994

In history's largest successful jewel theft, machine-gun toting robbers make off with over 45 million dollars worth of jewelry from the Cannes Carlton Hotel. The gendarmes later discover that the criminals were firing blanks.

1999

Sarah Jessica Parker, playing the fictional fashion chameleon Carrie Bradshaw, wears her infamous nameplate necklace for the first time during the second season of *Sex and the City*. Retailers selling knockoffs rejoice, for now anything SJP touches turns to gold.

2000

Robbers try to bash their way into London's Millennium Dome and steal 200 million UK pounds' worth of diamonds being exhibited by De Beers. Unbeknownst to the thieves, the police had been tipped off and worthless crystals were substituted for the jewels.

2002

Hollywood pop star and diva Jennifer Lopez popularizes colored diamonds with her much-photographed 6.1-carat pink diamond engagement ring given to her by actor Ben Affleck. She simultaneously releases a hit song that croons "Don't be fooled by the rocks that I got." Two years later, singer Marc Anthony tops the actor by ponying up an 8-carat number. But she's still Jenny from the block.

2004

Tyra Banks models the latest Victoria's Secret Fantasy Bra, which is encrusted with 112 carats of flashing diamonds and worth 10 million dollars. Now that's flaunting one's assets!

charm school fundamentals

Before you dive into the projects, it's essential that you spend some time studying the fundamentals: the tools, hardware, and metals that go into making beautiful things. After you have mastered the basics, you can expand your collection of DIY baubles past simple necklaces, bracelets, and earrings into more interesting, gemstyle-oriented jewels.

Tool Box for Your Jewel Box

You've bought the book and you've picked out some stones. Now, what else do you need to put it all together? Let's start by looking at the tools you'll need for making gorgeous jewelry.

JEWEL TOOLS

There are just four tools that you will need to complete the projects in this book: flat-nose pliers, round-nose pliers, cutters, and crimping pliers. (The word *nose* refers to the end of the tool, or its jaws.) These tools can be found at bead or craft stores or even at well-stocked hardware stores.

Flat-Nose Pliers
The jaws of these pliers are flat on the inside.

Round-Nose Pliers
The ends of these pliers are made up of two pointed metal cone-like rods that narrow at the tip.

Cutters
These have small, sharp blades at the end, used for cutting wire and findings.

Crimping Pliers
These professional crimping tools have two notches in the jaws for shaping and securing crimp beads.

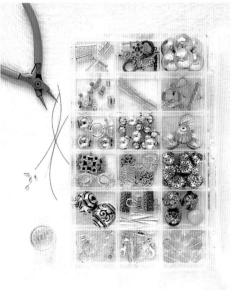

FINDINGS

The components in jewelry making that allow you to assemble, attach, and hold together your entire piece are called "findings." Below, I've outlined all the basic findings you'll need in order to complete the projects in this book. For more specific information, ask for help at your local bead store.

Clasps

Clasps allow you to open and close a piece of jewelry. Lobster claws, safety clasps, toggles, S-hooks, and tube/slide clasps are some of the most common.

Connectors

Connectors, such as jump rings (soldered and unsoldered), head pins, eye pins, and split rings, join the components of your piece of jewelry. Head pins can be bent and molded, and they can also dangle, in addition to many other uses.

Earring Findings

These are the pieces that go through the piercing in your earlobe, and they come in many different forms, including posts, ear wires (also called "French wires"), lever backs, and hoops. Select them carefully, because some people are very sensitive to certain metals (see "Glossary of Metals," page 19).

Clip-on earring findings have become more common in recent years and also more stylish. Most clip-ons have a loop in front to which you can attach an existing earring, chain, or decorated head or eye pin, making it easy to convert pierced earrings into clip-ons.

Wire

Jewelry wire is made in different colors and degrees of flexibility and strength. At the beginning you'll want to stock your tool box with small coils of wire in a variety of sizes. Good beading wire is actually made up of multiple tiny strands of flexible stainless steel wire twisted tightly together and coated with a nylon finish. It is available in diameters (meaning the width across the tip of flexible stringing wire) from about .010 to .026 inches (.026 being the thickest).

While I hesitate to endorse particular brands in this book, I will say that I have found Soft Flex to be the most sturdy, flexible, non-kinking, and trustworthy professional jewelry wire. All the pieces shown in this book were made using Softflex. It is more expensive than other jewelry wire, but I believe it is worth the additional cost. However, any similar beading wire will do.

When working with precious metal wire, you'll find that silver or gold are best for wire-working or wire-wrapping projects. Precious metal wire with "dead soft" *gauge* (a term meaning the thickness and, hence, the malleability, of metal wire) is the softest and most flexible for wire work, and it makes many projects a breeze. Again, it will take some practice before you can easily gauge your gauge.

Crimps

The most important technique you will learn from this book is crimping, which involves using a crimp bead or tube. Crimps are used to secure your clasp to your stringing wire. Don't underestimate these tiny metal cylindrical beads—they are truly a force to be reckoned with. Much like good double-sided tape at the Oscars, crimps keep everything firmly in place.

glossary of metals

In order to choose the right findings for your wearable masterpieces, you'll need to know which metals are best. Here are some basics, so you can work like a pro.

ALLOY: A mixture of metals.

GOLD FILLED: A mixture of real gold and a second metal. Significantly less expensive than real gold and very durable, they usually will not cause an allergic reaction.

PLATED: Gold- or silver-plated metals have an outer coat of real silver or gold over a base metal. The outer metal can scratch or chip off over time.

SOLID SILVER OR GOLD: Solid all the way through in either sterling silver or gold (any carat, usually 14, 18, or 22). The most expensive type of metal.

VERMEIL (pronounced "ver-may"): Solid sterling silver base with a thin 14-, 18-, or 22-carat gold electroplated finish.

style guide

Before you turn yourself loose and start creating your own cutting-edge looks, you'll also need to know about the standard jewelry lengths and styles. Here are some basic length and style illustrations to help guide you.

Jewelry style examples pictured from left to right are as follows: **(1)** drop earrings, triple-strand nested necklace in three lengths (choker, 15 to 16 inches; princess, 18 inches; and matinee, 20 to 22 inches), bracelets, and charm anklet; **(2)** hoop earrings and double-strand necklace with pendant; **(3)** chandelier earrings, lariat necklace, bangle bracelets, and cocktail ring; **(4)** chunky choker necklace; **(5)** post earrings, cuff bracelet, and rope length necklace (48 inches or longer). Not shown: opera length necklace (24 to 36 inches).

From chunky and irregular to petite and polished, gemstone beads come in many different shapes, sizes, and colors.

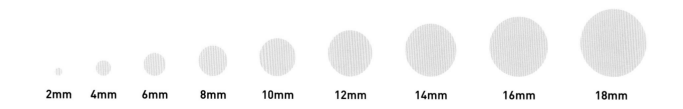

2mm 4mm 6mm 8mm 10mm 12mm 14mm 16mm 18mm

basic necklace assembly

This is it. You have learned about the basic tools and materials, and now it's time to try your hand at making something beautiful. So, gather your essential jewelry-making items: tools, beads and gemstones, wire, a margarita rocks no salt, findings. We're going to make a simple yet beautiful necklace that will be a perfect warm-up for the rest of the projects in this book. With this project, you will practice the basics—stringing, crimping, and adding a clasp. If you are already panicking and reconsidering taking that knitting class instead, stop. Rest assured, jewelry making is about to become a fun and fabulous part of your life.

Let's begin by making a 16-inch necklace, what I call a "relaxed choker." Comfort is key here—we are not making a tight-fitting, bejeweled dog collar, as much as Fifi might love it.

STRINGING

HOW TO

1. Take your beads and line them up to make sure that you have about 15½ inches of length (the clasp will make up the ½-inch difference). If your beads are not all the same color and you want to arrange them in a certain pattern or order, do so now. If you don't have enough beads, add a few beads in a similar or complementary color to each end of your necklace. Clear beads, or metal ones to match the clasp, also work well. You might want to use a bead board (see "Resources," page 119, for suppliers), which has several grooved lengths for laying out your beads and keeping them in place. (Some jewelry makers think that using a bead board is cheating, but we won't tell.)

2. Cut yourself some wire with your cutters. As a general rule, especially when you're just starting out, give yourself a few extra inches to work with on each side. For example, in order to have 3 extra inches on each side of a 16-inch necklace, cut about 22 inches of wire.

YOU WILL NEED

- 15 to 16 inches' worth of beads

- Approximately 20 inches of wire

- Cutters

- 2 crimp beads

- Clasp

- Flat-nose pliers

3. Start stringing! You can start from either the center or the end. If you want to end up with a central focal point such as a large bead or pendant, you'll find it easier to start in the center. To do so, anchor one end of your wire to your workspace, tray, or bead board (with Scotch tape, a binder clip, gum, or whatever you have lying around—the stickier and sturdier the better) and begin by stringing on the center bead. Don't worry about it sliding all the way down to the taped end; you'll recenter it later when you add the beads from the other side (see step 6 under "Adding a Clasp," below). Continue stringing on the rest of your beads. If you don't have a center bead for a focal point, you can simply string from left to right, or right to left, whichever way you swing—I mean *string*!

ADDING A CLASP: THE CRIMP-FLATTENING METHOD

Now comes the tricky part: once you have completed stringing all of your beads, it is time to add and secure half of a clasp to one end of the necklace.

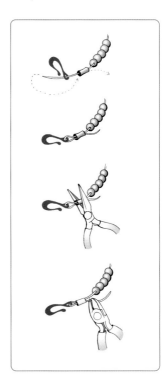

HOW TO

1. Slip one of the crimp beads onto the end of your beading wire.
(Try using your thumb to gently hold it in place while starting the next step.)

2. With your other hand, string on one half of your clasp set.

3. Take the end of the wire that has gone through your clasp around and back through the crimp toward the last bead on the necklace. Pull, tighten, and maneuver the crimp until it is snug between your clasp and the last bead.

4. Using your flat-nose pliers, firmly close down on the crimp until it crushes around and catches the wire. Tug on your clasp to make sure it is nice and tight. If the wire slides around at all, throw in the towel and go pour another margarita. *Kidding*, simply slide it off and start over with a new crimp bead.

5. Slide your cutters up in between the remaining wire and the crimp and cut off any excess wire.

6. On the other side of the necklace, add beads in the same order up to the crimp bead. Repeat the above crimping procedure and trim excess wire.

ADDING A CLASP: THE FOLD-OVER CRIMPING METHOD

Now that you've got the flattening method down, you're ready to learn an alternative crimping method, used by the pros. Of course, there is nothing wrong with using the previous method, and it makes for good beginner practice—but this second method has a prettier, cleaner finish.

If you have already finished the basic necklace, then you might want to start a new one, or just use some extra beads you've got lying around, in order to try out this method. All you really need is a few inches of wire, some crimp beads, and crimping pliers to learn and practice this technique, which you can use in all of your future jewelry projects.

First, let's examine those crimping pliers up close and personal. Looking carefully at the jaws, you will see two notches on the interior. Instead of flattening your crimp in the previously described barbaric way (well, it just doesn't seem all that ladylike!), you can use these notches to skillfully position your crimp bead to be dented and then folded over itself for additional security and all-around loveliness.

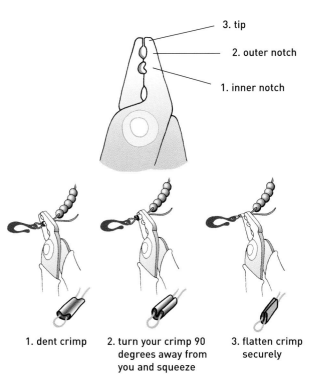

3. tip

2. outer notch

1. inner notch

1. dent crimp

2. turn your crimp 90 degrees away from you and squeeze

3. flatten crimp securely

HOW TO

1. After stringing the beads onto the wire, place your crimp bead on the end of your wire and follow steps 1 through 3 under "Adding a Clasp," opposite.

2. Position your crimping pliers around the crimp bead so that the crimp bead rests inside the smooth, oval-shaped inner notch on one of the jaws. The notch that will close directly over the crimp bead should be the one that appears to have a little bump or tooth inside it.

3. *Slowly* squeeze the handles so that the crimp bead is pinched between this notch. If you look closely at the crimp bead you should be able to see a dent being created through the center of it as you compress the handles.

4. Without turning the crimp bead, slide it and the wire up into the outer notch on the jaw. Then turn it 90 degrees so that the dent you have created is facing outward (instead of up) and away from your hand holding the tool.

5. *Slowly* squeeze down on the crimp bead again. Watch closely as the edges of the crimp bead fold over the dent toward each other and firmly close to form a neat, rounded cylindrical shape, locking in the wires.

This technique can be tricky to perform at first and requires a lot of practice. The part that frustrates many beginners is the step where you fold over the crimp bead in the second notch. However, if you work slowly and turn your crimp bead only 90 degrees so that the crimp bead is in the right place, it will close easily and seamlessly, yielding a cleanly folded and beautifully attached clasp.

WIRE-WRAPPING TECHNIQUE

I know you are fabulous and busy and eager to get started, but you definitely need to learn about wire wrapping in order to tackle many of the projects in the book. Do some quick yoga moves and slow down, sister.

Wire wrapping is the process of making a loop on top of a head pin or at the end of a piece of wire to create a connector from which to attach or dangle another stone or jewelry component. There are two types of loops you'll need to learn: a simple loop and a wrapped loop.

Simple Loop

As its name implies, this is the easiest and most common loop used in jewelry making.

SIMPLE LOOP

HOW TO

1. Using one hand, pinch the end tip of the wire using your round-nose pliers.

2. Holding your wire firm with your other hand (or with flat-nose pliers), turn the round-nose pliers *slowly* away from you, rolling the wire tip around the end of the pliers until it forms a closed loop.

3. To finish, position the pliers' tips just below the loop you have created and bend it backward 90 degrees, centering the loop above the rest of the wire. Now you have created a simple loop that can be gently opened and closed using flat-nose pliers in order to add or attach pieces.

YOU WILL NEED

- 2-inch piece of "dead soft" silver wire or thin head pin

- Round-nose pliers

Wrapped Loop

Now it's time for serious wire wrapping. With practice, you will find this technique easier and be able to give a more professional, finished look to your creations.

WRAPPED LOOP

snip

HOW TO

1. Making your loop about 1 inch below the tip of your wire, follow steps 1 and 2 in the instructions for making a simple loop, opposite, so that approximately 1 inch of wire sticks out past the loop.

2. Without adjusting the pliers' position after bending the wire, pull the wire up and all the way around the nose of your pliers in a 360-degree turn, going back to the same position, keeping your pliers steady and strong.

3. Take the remaining wire and wrap it tightly around the base of the wire loop, nestling it underneath until you have made a neat coil. Two or three wraps are usually plenty.

4. Using your cutters, trim any remaining wire that might be sticking out. If necessary, use your flat-nose pliers to smooth out your wrapped coils and pinch the end piece neatly toward the stem of the wire. Adjust or reshape your loop if it has gotten banged up in the wrapping process.

Tip: Try making a wrapped loop using a head pin with a large bead on it, to create a pendant with a bail (a loop used for hanging pendants or decorative pieces).

So there you have it—a beautiful necklace, maybe some wire-wrapped beads that can be used as charms, and lots of new skills. Ready to get your sparkle on?

YOU WILL NEED

- 1 thin head pin or 2-inch piece of "dead soft" silver wire

- Round-nose pliers

- Cutters

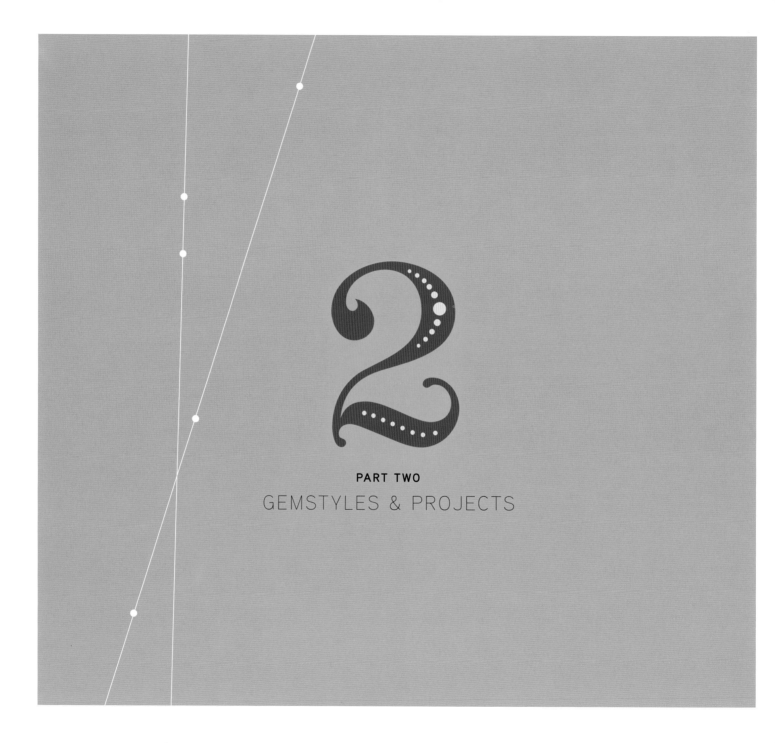

2

PART TWO

GEMSTYLES & PROJECTS

classic gemstyle

TIMELESS AND ELEGANT

**AUDREY HEPBURN
AS HOLLY GOLIGHTLY**

Tried and true, Classic Gemstyle evokes the elegance of the past without looking clichéd. *Like the little black dress or a plush cashmere cardigan, Classic Gemstyle bypasses trend yet always manages to nimbly scale the heights of fashion (even in 3-inch lizard pumps!). Classic gemstone jewelry, such as diamond studs, antique brooches, and tennis bracelets, might be considered safe choices, but the understated simplicity of their settings and design often serve to emphasize the intrinsic beauty of the stones themselves. You can't get much more* classic *than an exquisite diamond solitaire—unless it's a breathtaking string of identical luminous pearls.*

Pearls were the first "jewels" discovered by human beings and they have certainly withstood the test of time. Strung between emeralds by the ancient Egyptians, clustered with rubies and diamonds on Renaissance brooches, or fashioned into ropy loops at the House of Chanel, pearls are the ultimate classic.

Advancements in culturing technology in the 1920 and 1930s added to their popularity. Soon the pearl, formerly a luxury afforded only by the wealthy, had become an adornment for the masses. No worries if you couldn't afford the natural or cultured beauties; fabulous fakes began to proliferate in the market, and designers crafted glamorous pieces with bigger and bolder man-made pearls.

In the 1961 film *Breakfast at Tiffany's*, Audrey Hepburn as Holly Golightly wore a multistrand of grape-sized pearls while nibbling on pastries and pining over the goodies on display at the famed jewelry store. Her infectious joie de vivre and her spirited take on classic style overturned the notion that the traditional in fashion must be muted and staid. Holly signified an Everygirl's longing for sparkle and showed us how to shine in such timeless items as an impeccably cut shift and pristine white gloves, paired with the appropriate baubles, of course. For a tutorial in the classics, curl up in front of a DVD of *Breakfast at Tiffany's*—and don't forget the champagne.

not-your-grandmother's pearl necklace

Do you cherish your classic set of graduation or wedding pearls (the ones that are gathering dust in the bottom of your jewelry box)? Why not reinvent them by mixing in a glittering pile of colorful jewels? Adding one strand of semiprecious stones transforms your pearl choker into a brilliant wraparound or opera-length necklace. Don't be afraid to throw in vibrant, unexpected colors—everyone knows that pearls go with anything! We mixed in a strand of aqua-colored chalcedony rondels, as well as some small round silver accents.

HOW TO

1 ∷ If Granny's pearls are knotted, start by carefully cutting them apart with your cutters.

2 ∷ Experiment with the pearls and stones, using about 3 inches of wire, until you have a pattern you like. You may be tempted to do an "every other" type of pattern on this first project—if you do, make sure you have enough of each stone, or you may run out of one type and have too many of the other left over before you've finished. In making this necklace we used the following pattern: 2 pearls, 1 silver bead, 1 aqua stone, 1 silver bead.

3 ∷ Start your necklace by attaching half of the clasp with a crimp bead.

4 ∷ String on the beads in your selected sequence until your necklace is 32 inches long, or a length that you can wrap around your neck twice comfortably. You can start with any bead, but aim to end with the same one, if possible.

5 ∷ Attach the other half of the clasp with a crimp bead and trim any excess wire.

Variation: This necklace can also be worn long (unwrapped) or tied in a loose knot in front. To make it possible to tie it in a knot, leave a half inch of wire between your last bead and the crimp bead, which will allow the beads to spread out and reposition when you're tying the knot.

you will need

- Granny's pearls (at least 16 inches)

- Cutters

- 16 inches' worth of drilled stones

- About 45–50 small silver beads

- At least 32 inches of wire (thin, or .014 diameter, recommended for smaller lightweight stones), long enough to loop comfortably around your neck twice

- Clasp

- 2 crimp beads

- Flat-nose or crimping pliers

girly pearl necklace

With a few pearls left over from other projects, you can create this delicate "floating necklace," a soft and flattering design that uses crimp beads and clear wire so that the gems appear to be floating around your neck. While cool, lustrous white is always lovely, rosy pink pearls with gold accents radiate a warm glow and make your skin look dewy. This 16-inch necklace features seven sections, but you can vary your own depending on the number of leftover stones you have.

HOW TO

1 :: With your leftover pearls (or stones) and additional decorative bead findings, determine the pattern of each section that will repeat throughout this necklace. Placing decorative beads on each side of the pearl will enhance the look dramatically. Think ahead and make sure that you have an equal amount of empty space between each section of pearls and beads. For this 16-inch necklace I used 1¾ inches of space between each section of the pattern. I combined gold findings with large, pink, irregular freshwater pearls to make the piece more distinctive and feminine.

2 :: Using the crimp-flattening method (see "Adding a Clasp: the Crimp-Flattening Method," page 22), attach one half of your clasp to one end of the Invisiline. I used a delicate gold S-hook with a soldered jump ring on each side. It is important to use the crimp-flattening method for this project instead of the fold-over method because Invisiline is too thin to stay put in the fold-over process, and the flattened crimp beads become part of the "look" of this necklace. (Crimp beads are used throughout this piece to anchor the sections of bead pattern on their left and right sides so that they do not slide.) After the crimp bead, string on the first section of the bead pattern: gold bead, decorative finding, pearl, decorative finding, gold bead, followed by another flattened crimp bead.

you will need

- 7 pearls

- 14 small, round gold beads

- 14 additional decorative gold beads (different from the small, round gold beads mentioned above; referred to as *findings* in the instructions)

- At least 16 gold crimp beads

- 20 inches (or desired length) of Invisiline (or monofilament or any other transparent stringing line of .018 gauge or less)

- Clasp

- Flat-nose pliers

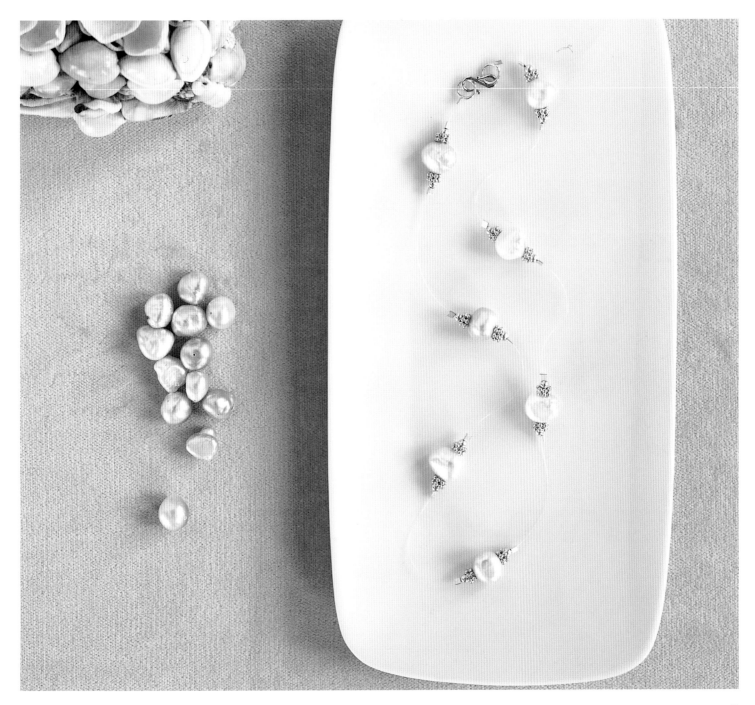

3 :: Leaving the predetermined space after the last crimp bead, add another crimp bead to start the next section of pattern, again finishing with a crimp bead. Repeat until your necklace has reached 16 inches (or your desired length) and end with a flattened crimp bead.

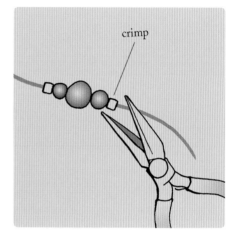

crimp

Variation: For a less formal, more asymmetrical style, try using a random and nonmatching pattern with uneven spacing throughout the piece. To achieve a sexy-sloppy layered look, you can attach additional nonmatching strands of varied lengths to the same piece. Do this by attaching the ends of the new strands to the same clasp using more crimp beads.

✳ knotty girl

There are times when knotting the string between gems seems more elegant or appropriate, but it's not a must when using pearls or heavier stones. In fact, knotted pieces often stretch over time, and the look can make a piece appear more formal than intended—and it takes time to do! But if you choose to knot, here's how to do it:

Silk cord is best, but you can also use nylon. Cut double the desired length of your final piece (to account for the knots). You will also need knotting tweezers, which are used to carefully form and move the knots into place. Having started your strand, determine how frequently you want the knots to occur (every other stone? every three?). Tie your first knot loosely around the end of your tweezers (or the pointy tip of a knotting needle) (illustration 1). Using the tweezers, slide the knot all the way down, as close to the stone as possible. Without tightening, slowly slide the tip of the tweezers out, and if there is any room left between the stone and the knot use your tweezers to pull the knot a touch closer (illustration 2). Then pull firmly on the cord to tighten it up. Repeat until you have finished knotting your whole strand.

illustration 1

illustration 2

YUMMY LEFTOVERS

*Here are some delicious ideas for your old trinkets
and hand-me-downs.*

- Turn an antique cameo brooch into a funky pendant with a
  simple jump ring (see photo).

- Choose a bright-colored, medium to large nugget stone
  and wrap it with leather or suede cord in either criss-cross
  or gift-wrap style and knot on top. Tie it around your wrist
  as a bracelet—a variation on the "All-Tied-Up Ribbon Cuff"
  project in the next chapter.

- Practice your wire-wrapping skills and dangle tiny gemstones in assorted colors from a skinny silver necklace
  chain.

- Convert your generic ribbed tank top into a sweet
  camisole by sewing a few pretty drilled stones or small
  antique buttons onto the strap or neckline.

- When you have only a couple of leftover stones from a necklace
  or bracelet project, use a head pin to attach them to ear posts
  or wires to make a pair of complementary earrings.

- Don't be afraid to alter the length of a hand-me-down
  piece, remove or add a pendant, change the clasp, or mix
  in some gemstones. Make it your own!

preppy gemstyle

FRESH AND BRIGHT

Despite its association with affluence, preppy has always been practical. In 1960, the young entrepreneurial socialite Lilly Pulitzer needed to design a uniform for the juice stand she had opened in Palm Beach, Florida. She chose a Day-Glo patterned cotton dress in order to camouflage the lemon, lime, orange, and pink grapefruit stains that were ruining her other clothing. Her juice was popular, but what customers really wanted was that dress. Soon after, super-bright colors and practical fabrics became de rigueur for resort clothing, and preppy fashion palettes never looked back.

In the 1970s and 1980s, preppy meant a slavish uniform of layered polos, whale embroidered cords, and pearls, but today's take on the style is based on color, wit, and crisp and playful jewels that recall Lilly's days in the sun. You don't need to summer on Nantucket to show off Preppy Gemstyle. Modern preppy is a tongue-in-chic riff on country club and prep school stylings without being a head-to-toe look.

Oversized floral or dome-shaped studs can make a tailored oxford shirt or crisp khakis look fresh and pretty. Toss on an armful of bright Bakelite bangles for a look that says "cocktails at the club." If bangles aren't your thing, try a monogrammed gold bracelet or play with thick grosgrain ribbon to make watchbands and bracelets like the "All-Tied-Up Ribbon Cuff" on page 38.

When choosing colored stones, look for pink rose quartz, red coral, bright-green peridot, or lepidiolite (a purply pink opaque gem). Or go for these same fun hues in lacquered and glass beads. And don't forget that Preppy Gemstyle embraces the nostalgic—treasures handed down from one generation to the next, including lockets, signet and school rings, and bracelets loaded with charms gathered on Great-Aunt Chessie's Grand Tour.

Lots of preppy clothes were originally designed for sporting—hence their comfort and practicality. Outdoorsy, clean lines and strong colors are meant to play all day and still look fresh and spiffy for cocktail hour at the yacht club. It goes without saying that swinging beads and chandelier earrings don't usually work with these no-nonsense fashions. Think lime-green chrysoprase chokers or sweet gold huggies (baby hoop earrings) instead. Anchors aweigh!

think pink...
and green necklace

Whether you're facing the first day at boarding school or the Fourth of July at the Vineyard, bright-colored ribbon is always a perfect choice in the preppy world. Satin ribbon paired with preppy pink and green stones makes a sweet, pretty necklace (I used smooth, round rose quartz and aventurine gems here). Tie it up tight for a fun choker or leave it long and loose for a more elegant piece. Looking for a playful, feminine variation? Turn it around and wear the bow in front.

HOW TO

1 :: Start by attaching the end of your jewelry wire to one jump ring with a crimp bead using the fold-over crimping method (see "Adding a Clasp: the Fold-Over Crimping Method," page 23), and trim any excess wire. (The jump ring is used instead of a traditional clasp.)

2 :: String on your stones in alternating order (or in another pattern) until the necklace reaches 16 inches and attach the second jump ring with a crimp bead at the end of your wire. Trim any excess wire. When open, this will look like a full-length necklace with two hoops on the ends instead of a clasp.

3 :: Cut 2 pieces of ribbon and tie (or sew) one end of each piece to a respective jump ring. To close the necklace, tie the 2 ribbons together in a bow. Wear the bow in back or in front.

Variation: Cut a single long piece of ribbon, thread it through both jump rings, and tie in a bow; it can be tied tight for choker length or loose for a longer style, and worn in front or in back.

Aren't you pretty! Time to tie one on.

all-tied-up ribbon cuff

Even if you can't thread a needle without spilling blood, trust me—if I can tackle this sewing project, so can you. A chunky nugget stone funks up this clean, sporty ribbon cuff. Casual, translucent stones in bright colors are great for day, but you can also sew deep plum, blue, or iridescent gray gems onto satin or velvet for a sultry evening look.

HOW TO

1 :: Start by measuring the ribbon for your wrist. You will want to cut the ribbon where it overlaps with the other side by approximately 1 inch (to accommodate the Velcro closure). If your wrist is 7 inches around, cut 8 inches of ribbon.

2 :: Test your stone to make sure that the needle will pass through the drill hole (if not, you will have to select another stone or find a smaller needle).

3 :: Cut about 12 to 16 inches of thread. Start by tying a big, sturdy knot 2 inches from the end of your thread. Now, thread your needle (hope you didn't have too many double espressos this morning).

4 :: Determine the exact spot where you want to attach your stone. Lay the ribbon flat on your table and place the stone in the spot, so that the drill holes are in a horizontal line. With a pencil or fine-tip pen, make a tiny mark on the ribbon directly below the drill holes on each side of the stone.

5 :: Starting on the underside of the ribbon, pierce one of the marked spots with your needle and push it through until your thread tugs against the knot beneath the ribbon. Pass your needle through the drill hole of the stone and pull out the other side until taut. Puncture the second marked spot on the other side of the stone and push the needle down through the ribbon, pulling gently until taut. Push the needle back up through the ribbon in a spot just a hair over from the spot you just pulled through and repeat the procedure in reverse, going back through the stone and down through the ribbon on the other side.

you will need

- Approximately 10 inches of wide ribbon (preferably grosgrain)

- Scissors

- 1 beautiful, drilled stone nugget (or other shape)

- Needle and thread (matching the color of your *stone*, not the ribbon)

- Pencil or fine-tip pen

- 3 inches of heavy-duty adhesive Velcro

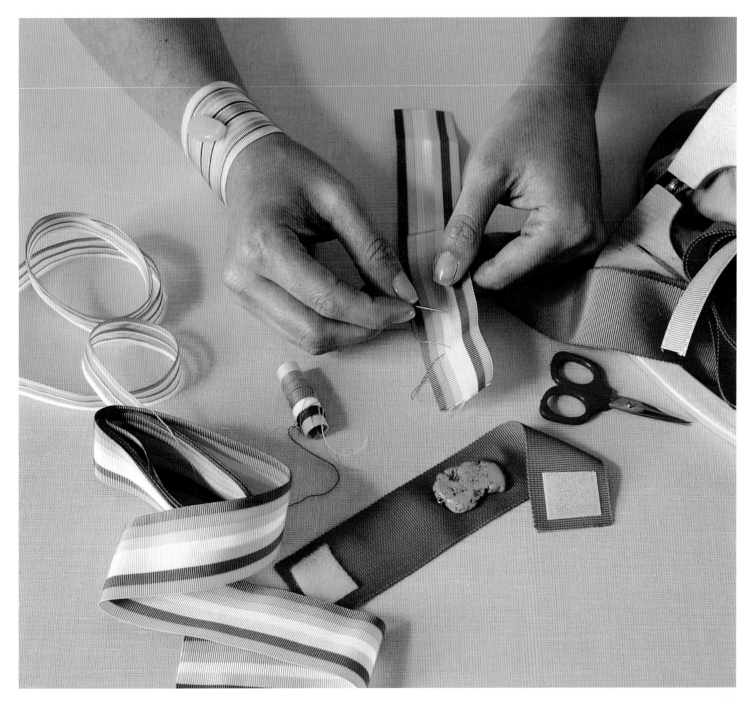

6 :: Repeat about 5 times on each side of the stone, ending on the side you started. Tie your remaining thread together with the 2 inches left hanging from your original knot.

7 :: Cut and attach a neat square of Velcro to the outside of one end of the ribbon and the inside of the other end.

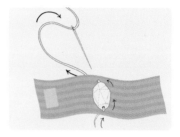

Tip: If your needle does not fit into the drill hole of the stone, try pushing a head pin through the drill hole and curling both ends (see "Simple Loop," page 24). Then sew through those loops instead of directly through the stone itself.

ribbon belt

This is an easy and fun "leftovers" project—and one you will really use! If you bought a yard or two of pretty ribbon to make your ribbon bracelet, then chances are that you have enough remaining to make a charming prepster belt.

HOW TO

Follow the instructions for the ribbon cuff necklace on the previous pages (minus the stone), simply making it a lot longer. Don't forget: the *outside* of one end of the ribbon attaches to the *inside* of the other end.

YOU WILL NEED

- Ribbon, enough to go around the waist of your blue jeans plus 1 to 2 inches

- 1 to 2 inches of heavy-duty adhesive Velcro

bright idea

PLAYING WITH MATCHES

Not sure when to wear jewelry sets and when to mix it up? You don't want to get burned by excess, nor do you want to let your sparkle fizzle. In general, it's best to stick with one bold statement piece or artfully combine a group of more balanced jewels. Traditionally, matched "suites" of jewelry have been reserved for dressed-up occasions, but even this rule is not set in stone. The guideline you'll find most useful is simple: just don't overdo it.

For example, pearl sets always look ladylike, whether paired with jeans and pretty slingbacks or your favorite slinky wrap dress. But refrain from donning your pearl studs, pearl choker, pearl brooch, and pearl bracelet all at once—unless you work for Mikimoto.

Or, let's say you are going for a funky boho look with long ropes of African amber. No need to find something identical for your lobes and wrists. Big, fun necklaces are often enough on their own and don't require a matching ensemble to complete the look. Can't live without earrings? Small studs—with real or faux gemstones—are an attractive and understated choice to wear with dramatic necklaces. Stylish gold baby hoops might complement the rich hue of your necklace without matching exactly. The same goes for simple but elegant citrine studs or decorative posts.

On the other hand, if a layered gypsy look is your thing, then wearing matching jewels *and then some* might express your personal style. If minimalist chic is more your vibe, then matching sets of jewelry might seem gaudy and unnecessarily ostentatious. Unless, of course it is your special night and piling on the sparkle makes you feel like the belle of the ball—in that case, don't forget your tiara!

ultra-chic gemstyle

SLEEK AND STYLISH

**DIANA VREELAND
"THE ORACLE"**

Perhaps no other woman has epitomized ultra-chic style more than the legendary fashion editor Diana Vreeland. Relying on her magnificent wit and flamboyance, Vreeland ascended to the top of the fashion heap, serving as fashion editor at Harper's Bazaar, *editor-in-chief of* Vogue, *and finally curator for the Metropolitan Museum of Art's Costume Institute. She punched up her exquisitely tailored clothing with eccentric, oversized jewelry—bangles, huge pendant necklaces, multiple rings, and pins. Vreeland knew that an ultra-chic jewelry wardrobe includes a cache of timeless, valuable* objets *that are spiced up each season with the addition of glam, inventive pieces.*

Like Vreeland, today's ultra-chic woman not only possesses an up-to-the minute knowledge of runway styles but also has a sixth sense about what will come next and what's out of mode. She follows the fashion pages with a keen eye, yet she is no designer's pawn. Ultra-chic women experiment with cutting-edge looks well before their trickled-down versions receive the approval of the mainstream, confidently mixing items and making it all appear so effortless.

If you're going for Ultra-Chic Gemstyle, gold—especially the glowing, supple quality of 18-carat gold—is always appropriate. Brushed gold looks and feels decadent and pricey, though it often isn't. Pair this precious metal with sumptuous stones in dark blue—a shade that is less ubiquitous than the tender blues of turquoise and aquamarine. Can't splurge on blue sapphire? Explore the deep-sea hues of lapis, tanzanites, and iolites. And dark and daring jet-black onyx and smoky topaz lend a mysterious and sexy vibe to ultra-chic jewelry.

On the other end of the spectrum there are diamonds, which never go out of style. Although they are not usually suitable for DIY gem projects, diamond pieces can be thrown on with almost anything for extra wattage. Don't be afraid to mix fine jewelry and serious stones with *bijoux de fantasie*—daring, current fashion pieces. Take a cue from Vreeland, who took risks and deftly wore the in, the outré, and the outrageous: "Never fear being vulgar, just boring."

the ultimate accessory necklace

For this project, I asked Alison Nichols, senior accessories editor at Glamour magazine,
to try her hand at designing jewelry at the Femmegems NoLita boutique. Naturally,
Ali sauntered into the shop and selected the most offbeat yet perfect strands to combine
into a fun and chic necklace, announcing, "I want thick, nested, organic-looking, brightly
colored beads stacked into a monstrous and fantastic necklace. I want the unexpected!"
And that's exactly what she created. Feel free to substitute your own strands of beads,
but here's how to duplicate this editorial darling.

Note: Making a nested multistrand necklace like this one looks easy, and, in fact, it is—if you are patient. This basic assembly concept is somewhat obvious: each successive strand is longer than the one nested inside it. However, there is no rule governing how much additional length will make each strand sit right. Other factors, such as bead size, shape, and even the wearer's collarbones, will affect the final fit.

HOW TO

1 :: With slide clasps, the bottom loop on one side connects with the top loop on the other side. Examine the clasp when it is detached. The mushroom cap ends on a slide clasp should always be facing the opposite direction when open.

2 :: Attach the wire with a crimp bead to the top loop at one end of the clasp. String on any end beads you may have chosen (Ali used a few purple glass beads to add a decorative, contrasting touch in the back) and then add the shortest/inner strand of beads. Adjust the strand to fit as tightly as is comfortable before closing it up with a crimp bead on the other side of the clasp.

3 :: Using the second, third, and fourth strands, repeat the process. However, after each strand is strung (from top to bottom), and before you tighten the final crimp bead, you must try on the necklace and make sure that it sits flat below the previous strand. If it bunches the strand above it or creates a gaping space between the two, then slide off the crimp bead and adjust as needed by adding or removing a few beads. Remember to leave space for your decorative end beads, if you have used them.

Be sure that one of the mushroom cap ends on your slide clasp faces up, and the other faces down.

you will need

- 4-strand slide clasp

- At least 75 inches of stringing wire

- At least 8 crimp beads

- 12 to 24 end beads in a complementary color of your choice, for additional length if necessary (see photo)

- 16-inch strand of green amazonite faceted stones (about 10mm each)

- 20 inches of oversized gold potato pearls

- 24 inches of white or ivory "bone" beads (fat rondel shape)

- 28 inches of jumbo lacquered faux coral balls (about 22mm each)

- Crimping pliers

- Cutters

ONE ITEM WORN THREE WAYS:

A beautiful brooch on a jacket, a strand of pearls, and a clutch handbag.

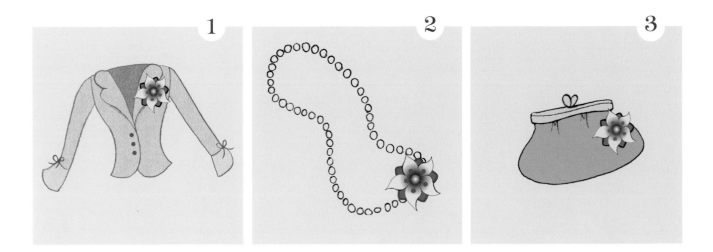

peek inside

Here is what Ali had to say about her treasures:

"These earrings are by Renne Lewis, one of my favorite designers ever. I love that they don't match, an unusual element in fine jewelry . . . and they are two of my favorite colors, pink and green!

"Beach-inspired jewelry is so fun. This Simon Tu pin uses delicious organic, natural-looking stones.

"I am a big fan of gold jewelry and this Balboa pendant goes with everything . . . white jeans in the summer or over a cashmere sweater in the winter. Lucky me—these three items were all gifts from the designers.

"I bought these rings on the street in Havana, Cuba, for three dollars. I adore them because they look huge on my long, skinny hands and reminds me of my fascinating tropical journey."

chain, chain, chain earrings

OK, let's make some earrings. Assuming you own the basics—pearl studs, maybe even diamond ones too, pretty hoops, and a sexy pair of monster chandeliers—why don't we try something in between? Working with gold and silver chain might seem intimidating, but getting comfortable with making bales and wire wrapping will expand your jewelry-making options and take your expertise to a new level. And these chain and gem earrings, which include strawberry quartz beads, pearls, and crystal beads, certainly look more designer than DIY. Practice, practice, practice makes perfect!

HOW TO

1 :: Cut (or buy a precut) piece of 4-inch chain in half so that you have 2 equal pieces to start with.

2 :: Hold the chain up to one of the ear wires and determine how long you want the overall earring to be. (Adjust these instructions according to your chosen length.)

3 :: Using a head pin, create a simple loop with round-nose pliers (see "Simple Loop," page 24) on 2 each of the 3 types of stones (for a total of 6) and leave rolled ends open slightly for attachment purposes.

4 :: The number of links in your chain depends on what type of chain you chose. Counting all of the links, attach your first stone approximately a third of the way down the chain. Do this by opening your loop just enough to slip it onto the selected link in the chain and then closing firmly with flat-nose pliers. Attach the rest of the stones the same way, equally spaced down the chain, attaching the last one to the very last link, anchoring the earring.

you will need

- Cutters

- Approximately 4 inches of small linked silver chain

- 1 pair silver ear wires

- 6 head pins (preferably with ball ends)

- Round-nose pliers

- 4 each of 3 different types of beads and gems

- Flat-nose pliers

5 :: With your flat-nose pliers, slightly open the loop on the bottom of the ear wire. Gripping the second link down from the top of your chain, dangle and slip the first (top) chain link onto the open loop of the ear wire. Close firmly with the pliers to finish.

6 :: Repeat steps 3 through 5 to assemble the matching earring.

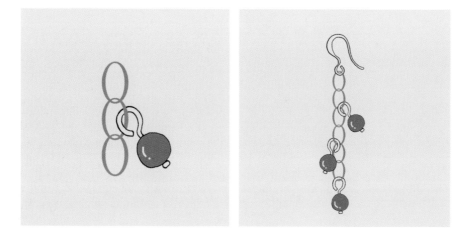

bridal gemstyle

SWEET AND FESTIVE

"Here comes the bride, all dressed in white. . ." Or so it used to be. Just as bridal dresses have gone from old fashioned, full-skirted, floor-length numbers to chic little confections gracing the pages of fashion rags, bridal gems have also become ultra stylish. But whether your dress is a classic Princess Diana–inspired gown with a football field of lace or a skimpy slip for a barefoot beach ceremony, bridal baubles have one thing in common: they make you (and your bridesmaids) sparkle on that special day. Sure, that twinkling new rock on your left hand speaks for itself, but an elegant décolleté dress and exquisite hair and makeup deserve exceptional jewelry. Just call it icing on the wedding cake.

Choices, choices. Hawaii or hometown? A-line or empire? Satin or silk? Fat pearl drops or dazzling bejeweled chandeliers? For decades pearls have been the obvious answer for formal weddings, but many brides nowadays are turning up the bling—with cubic zirconium (feel free to substitute the real thing if you are so blessed!); the plump shape of baby teardrops or oversized pear-cut stones looks über elegant with upswept hair. For an island destination wedding, why not try layers of pink conch shells or twists of fiery branch coral to add zing to an understated frock? And as for "something old, something new, something borrowed . . ." How about something *aquamarine*? A faceted lariat with a dangling pearl cluster would be subtly elegant.

When choosing jewelry for the bridesmaids, use color as a cue. Will your best gals be carrying bouquets of sweetheart pink roses or cream-colored lilies of the valley? Selecting beads or semiprecious jewels in tones that complement your floral choices will ensure a look that is feminine and put together. If your country-themed nuptials dictate cheerful golden sunflowers, add citrines or orange carnelian to the mix of gems. Bridesmaids always appreciate wearing something that they can use again. The teardrop necklace in this chapter is one item that they will happily throw on with a tank or a little black dress after your wedding.

Wondering what to give your bridesmaids as gifts? Go for something that captures their individual beauty. If your best friend's azure eyes simply glow when she wears blue, make her a pair of dangly blue topaz earrings. Or create a black onyx choker for the tomboy who has blossomed into a smoldering diva. Or, throw a jewelry-making fete for the bridesmaids a few days before the wedding to introduce the members of the wedding party and ensure that your big day will be a sparkling occasion!

it's-my-party teardrop necklace

Don't cry if the selection of wedding jewels at your local boutique leaves you cold. This graceful looped necklace is sure to shine on pretty, bare shoulders. Any shape or color stones can be substituted for the ones listed in the directions.

HOW TO

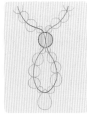

1 :: Cut your length of wire. For this project you will cut approximately 5 inches more than your desired fitting length (to be used to make the loop), not including the extra inches of wire you will need for the ends.

2 :: This is a piece that is easier to make by beginning in the center. Start by securing one end of the wire with tape. At the other end, string on the section of beads that will be your looped center piece (don't worry about making the loop itself yet): from left to right, string 1 medium lavender, 1 small purple, 3 medium lavender, 1 small round gold, amethyst teardrop (centerpiece), 1 small round gold, 3 medium lavender, 1 small purple. You will *not* need to string on the last medium lavender bead to mirror the first one you strung (see illustration).

3 :: Take the end of your wire and thread it back through the first bead you put on. This will transform the first bead into the top of the loop. Now string on the beads that will become one side of the necklace, starting at the bottom by the loop you have created and continuing up the spot where the clasp will go. Close that side temporarily with tape.

4 :: Untape the other side and hold up both ends of your necklace, which should have taken on its final looped shape, minus all the pretty gems on one side. Complete it by stringing the matching pattern of beads on the other side, right down to your loop. Before you add the clasp, try on the unfinished necklace and make length adjustments by adding or removing a few beads from each side. Then close using crimp beads and a clasp, and off to the church you go!

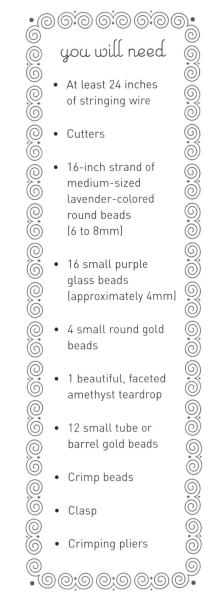

you will need

- At least 24 inches of stringing wire

- Cutters

- 16-inch strand of medium-sized lavender-colored round beads (6 to 8mm)

- 16 small purple glass beads (approximately 4mm)

- 4 small round gold beads

- 1 beautiful, faceted amethyst teardrop

- 12 small tube or barrel gold beads

- Crimp beads

- Clasp

- Crimping pliers

bejeweled bridesmaid party

What's better than bubbly and caviar? Bubbly and sparkles, of course! Why not throw a jewelry-making bridal shower for the lady of honor, or, if you're the one strolling down the aisle, thank your bridal party by organizing a jewelry-designing fete. Color-coordinated pieces can be worn at the wedding, and nothing will butter up your new mother-in-law better than a little bling! Here's how to throw a bridesmaids' party that rocks.

HOW TO

ONE MONTH AHEAD: Send out invites marked "The Bejeweled Bridesmaid Party." (This is a perfect opportunity to introduce your color scheme for the wedding, by the way.)

ONE WEEK AHEAD: Gather lots of pretty gems, beads, and findings for your guests to choose from. Make sure you have enough sets of tools so that the guests can work simultaneously. If the jewels are for the wedding, choose color-coordinated stones, but don't worry about selecting a particular design. Let the bridal party members express their personal style through their own designs.

THE DAY BEFORE: Display your gems and findings on pretty trays or in baskets. Piles of clasps and beads look nicer in little cups or dishes—anything from porcelain bowls to martini glasses can work.

Help guests distinguish their beverage glasses by creating "Stemgems Wineglass Markers" (see page 58) that they can take home as party favors, or supply materials for them to make their own as a starter project.

Create a workstation for each guest and supply it with the basics—clasps, crimp beads, wire, tape—and locate it within reach of essential tools such as pliers.

Check to make sure that you have enough lighting: low lights, big drinks, and tiny drill holes do not mix well. (Worried about your nails? Save the manicures for the day after the party.)

Prepare or purchase food and drinks. Keep food simple and small; savory finger foods are always a hit (honestly, show me a girl who doesn't like the occasional pig-in-a-blanket!). Stock up on plenty of sparkling water, juices, and soft drinks for those who prefer not to indulge. Buy flowers in your color scheme to add to the special-occasion atmosphere.

A FEW HOURS AHEAD: Make a signature drink and refrigerate. Toss a few slices of lemon into a pretty water pitcher.

JUST BEFORE THE PARTY: Set out flowers, food, and drinks on a surface other than your main work table.

Once your guests arrive, put on some fun, jewelry-themed tunes (see "Rock Songs," below) and get your collective sparkles on!

rock songs

Too much sparkle is never enough! "Rock" your party by playing these songs at your jewelry-making fest. While you're at it, why not burn them onto a CD and hand out copies as party favors?

"Diamonds Are a Girl's Best Friend" – MARILYN MONROE

"Diamonds on the Soles of Her Shoes" – PAUL SIMON

"Jenny from the Block" – J. LO

"Thru the Eyes of Ruby" – THE SMASHING PUMPKINS

"Gold Dust Woman" – FLEETWOOD MAC

"Emerald City" – TEENA MARIE

"Gold Finger" – TOM JONES

"Platinum Bells" – DESTINY'S CHILD

"Shine on You Crazy Diamond" – PINK FLOYD

"Gold Rush" – SNOOP DOGG

"Ruby Tuesday" – ROLLING STONES

"Heart of Gold" – NEIL YOUNG

"Rhinestone Cowboy" – GLEN CAMPBELL

"Sapphire Bullets of Pure Love" – THEY MIGHT BE GIANTS

"Lucy in the Sky with Diamonds" – THE BEATLES

"Silver Threads and Golden Needles" – JOHNNY CASH

"Ruby Don't Take Your Love Away from Me" – KENNY ROGERS

"Diamonds and Pearls" – PRINCE

"Diamond Life" – SADE

el sangria sparkler

Sangria is a festive, colorful drink that goes well with tasty appetizers and other yummy munchies. There's no need to raid the cellar for your finest—a decent red table wine will do just fine. Don't be afraid to make it nice and fruity—pear, kiwi, and tropical fruit can all be used instead of (or in addition to) peaches. The recipe below will serve 6.

HOW TO

1 :: Wash peaches and apples and cut into medium-sized chunks or slices.

2 :: Pour the wine into a pretty pitcher, add the sugar, and stir to dissolve.

3 :: Wash the oranges and squeeze out the juice. Add juice to the pitcher. Save a long strip of the orange peel to use as a garnish.

4 :: Sangria should always be served chilled, so pop it in the fridge at least 2 hours before your guests are due to arrive.

5 :: To serve, pour over ice with a splash of seltzer or soda to taste. Decorate each glass with a bit of orange peel.

Variation: Feel free to experiment by adding liquors such as rum or vodka, or you can dilute the alcohol content by using more juice and ice cubes. If you do add spirits and find the results irresistible, make sure your guests have a safe ride home, or take a long siesta after the party.

YOU WILL NEED

- 2 peaches
- 2 apples
- 1 bottle of red wine
- 5 teaspoons sugar
- 2 oranges
- Seltzer or lemon-lime soda

stemgems wineglass markers

Don't rely on lipstick stains to figure out whose glass is whose. Get your guests' jewelry-making skills warmed up with this fun project. These jeweled wineglass markers will thwart beverage-related confusion no matter how many drinks they have had. This project uses an earring hoop to loop around the stem of the glass.

HOW TO

1 :: Assign a bead to each glass. Next you will make the connecting device from which it will dangle.

2 :: Push a head pin through a bead to create your stemgem, or bead charm. At the end of the pin, make a wire-wrapped loop using round-nose pliers, and trim with cutters (see "Wrapped Loop," page 25). Repeat for each separate bead.

3 :: After you have made all of your bead charms, open the earring hoops gently.

4 :: Using round-nose pliers, bend the tip of the hoop wire up 90 degrees. Slip the wrapped loop of your gem onto the hoop and then place the hoop around the glass stem. Close by tucking the bent end of the hoop into its opposite loop.

you will need

- Several different beads or stones (1 per glass)

- Head pins (1 per glass)

- Round-nose pliers

- Cutters

- Flexible medium-size earring hoops (1 per glass)

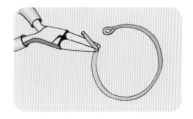

Variation: If you haven't mastered wire-wrapped loops yet, a simple loop will work just as well.

LINDSAY'S WEDDING

My own "country casual" nuptials were held outdoors in early fall in Southampton, New York. The day before the wedding, at a ladies' lunch, I armed my girlfriends with a few sparkles that I had designed. I wanted to present my best gals with necklaces and earrings that, much like their dresses and shoes—flirty lime-green strapless cocktail dresses with a soft ruffled hem and sassy gold kitten-heeled sandals—would truly be wearable after the big day.

Using green and gold for inspiration, I created necklaces with triple-strand twists of light- and dark-green freshwater pearls, peridot briolettes, and sprinklings of tiny brass and gold beads, which really made them gleam. The necklaces can be twisted tightly for a formal look or worn loosely overlapping for a sexy, casual style. For their earrings, I designed simple drops of double green and gold pearls that dangled from gold posts to give them a little movement. A recent sighting of one of my bridesmaids wearing her necklace with a feisty gold tank reassures me of the elegant but fun staying power of these gems—although I can't say as much for their shoes, which were destroyed by an epic downpour before the reception!

from black tie to easy breezy

From the engraving on the invitations to the vintage of the bubbly, you've deliberated over every detail of the wedding, so why breeze over the bijoux? Pearls are the bridal default, but so many other gems can give your look a more personal stamp (and make the photographs pop!). The deluxe mixture of Swarovski crystals, smoky topaz, and chocolaty pearls is just right for a grand cathedral procession. A stroll through the dunes, on the other hand, calls for carefree jewelry, such as this necklace made of faux shell branches.

party girl gemstyle

SEXY AND FLIRTATIOUS

MARILYN MONROE

Whether shaking that booty or strutting down the red carpet, a babe with Party Girl Gemstyle dresses to get noticed. She's dazzling, feminine, and a little bit audacious. She favors shimmering, touchable evening fabrics like satin, silk velvet, and chiffon that demand twinkling jewels. She's not shy about accessorizing for a big event—no heels are high enough and no rock big enough. And yes, diamonds really are a girl's best friend. As party girl Marilyn Monroe purred in Gentlemen Prefer Blondes, *"Talk to me, Harry Winston, tell me all about it."*

To achieve this festive, playful, and thoroughly feminine look on a budget, there's nothing wrong with going for a little cubic zirconium—we won't tell. Look-at-me settings include chandeliers, cluster drop earrings, tassels, and hoops encrusted inside and out with bright jewels. Obvious fakes too, like the "Extreme Makeover Earrings" featured in this chapter, look fun and flirty. A choker can flatter your exposed neck and shoulders, and an elegant wreath necklace illuminates the face while longer cascades show off a plunging neckline. To indulge your inner party girl, you might even use gemstone clips to tame your tousled bed head or grace your sleek upsweep with a delicate circlet.

You needn't drop the rocks after hours when you slip into something more comfortable. Sensual, rich-colored stones smolder at a party for two. Layer on mouthwatering watermelon and rainbow tourmalines. Sultry deep-purple amethysts or pink sapphires will make hearts thump and your pout shimmer when paired with a swipe of matching lip gloss. And don't hesitate to include sparkle in unexpected places. Glue on a temporary jewel above your lips, à la Cindy Crawford's infamous beauty mark, or hide one on your hipbone. Or slip on the bejeweled "Kicky Knickers" you will find in this chapter. Treasure hunt, anyone?

Don't fret if the Party Girl Gemstyle seems out of reach. Even if you are an exhausted mom, try throwing on a pretty skirt, some kitten heels, and two of your favorite sparklers. See if that doesn't put you into a more festive mood—even if the "event" ends up taking place with your husband in the kitchen after the kids hit the sack!

JEWELRY THAT TAKES YOU FROM WORK TO PARTY TO DINNER

It's 7:00 A.M., and a quick glance at your organizer reveals a full lineup for the day: client meeting at noon, cocktails with the girls after work, and a late dinner with your new man. So many commitments, yet zero time for a wardrobe change. Solution? Use your jewels!

Instead of stuffing an alternate outfit into your bag (yikes!), simply put on a skirted suit over a silky camisole or fluttery blouse, add pearls for that client meeting, and stash a few evening-style baubles in your makeup bag. After work, unbutton your blazer and remove your client-privileged pearls. Replace with a twirling pair of shimmery chandelier earrings and an oversized cocktail ring. Later on, when you're headed out for dinner à deux, pull your hair up into a swanky do, peel off that suit jacket, and ditch the big ring (after all, you don't want to give him jitters on the third date). Add a thick tortoise cuff for unexpected sex appeal, or toss on a few jingling bangles to keep the mood light. For a look that'll carry you to the boudoir, try a sweet but sexy lariat that will draw his eyes toward your low neckline. If you're still together when the lights go down, avoid injuries by leaving those chandeliers on the bedside table.

kicky knickers

Come on down off the bar, party girl, and let's take a look in your undies drawer. Those granny panties deserve a makeover, so why not sew on a few fun gemstones? Add just a couple in one corner or load on the stones and really make them twinkle. Next time you are up there dancing on the bar, you'll be sporting extra sparkle in case someone sneaks a peek. If you completed the "All-Tied-Up Ribbon Cuff" project (page 38), then this will be a piece of cheesecake.

HOW TO

1 :: Start by laying out your stones to determine their placement on the panties. You'll be sewing them on in a flower pattern, with one bead as the center, and the rest as the flower petals. Before you begin sewing, make sure you can get your needle through each of the stones that you have selected. If not, find a thinner needle or stones with bigger drill holes.

2 :: Double your thread and make a large knot at the end to prevent your first stitch from pulling through.

3 :: Determine the points in the material that are *right* below the drill holes, exactly where you want the center flower stone to sit. From underneath, puncture the panty material with your needle in the determined spot and pull the thread through.

4 :: Pass your needle through the hole in the stone, down into the material, and back up several times, until it is firmly sewn onto its spot. Finish with your needle on the inside, in the spot where you started, tie the thread ends together in a few double knots, and trim.

5 :: Repeat steps 2 through 4 to affix the other stones around the first, in the shape of a flower.

Tip: Maybe you throw those leopard print thongs straight into the machine, but I would suggest hand washing these babies. No party girl risks losing her jewels.

you will need

- 5 drilled stones

- 1 pair of panties (preferably cotton or a thicker synthetic; avoid sheers and lace)

- Needle and thread (to match the color of the panties)

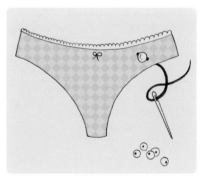

THE ROCKS THAT YOU GOT

extreme makeover earrings

It's time to dig deep in that jewelry box for old pieces in desperate need of a new look. Don't pass over the stuff you haven't touched since tenth grade. Odd ornaments from the past can look fabulous today. That weird enameled pin your Aunt Gladys gave you? It might look sexy hanging from a few strands of sparkly black onyx. That pair of Indian fringe earrings that haven't seen daylight in a decade? Put them on! Now!

When I excavated my jewel box for this project, I almost bypassed my old silver "spaceship necklace" (as I have lovingly called it for years). Then it occurred to me that it might be perfect material for a makeover: the wacky graduated fabric ball components could be fun to wear with '80s flair!

To start, I examined the piece's attachment methods. The ball beads were not strung on wire, so there was nothing to cut open. They were connected to each other via head pins looped together from end to end. I decided to take the 6 smallest beads from the back of the necklace (3 from each side of the clasp) and deconstruct them in order to turn them into earrings.

Using flat-nose pliers, I opened the loop on the end of the first bead, slipped it out of its clasp connector, and then reclosed it. Three beads down, I opened that bead's loop and slipped it out of its attachment. Now I had a section of three silver beads looped together by simple looped head pins. I then added a dangling stone to the bottom bead for a more-*sexy*, less–*Star Wars* look. Using a thin head pin, I wire wrapped a pretty orange carnelian faceted teardrop. I then attached it by opening up the bottom loop on the silver bead and sliding it on, then closing it (see "Wire-Wrapping Technique," page 24).

Finally it was time to add a pierced earring finding. I decided to stick with the vertical round feel of the three stacked beads and add a small hoop, which can be pulled apart gently and has natural resistance. I slipped it through the existing loop on top of the bead, and then closed it by bending its pointy back end upward 90 degrees. Once it's been pushed through the earlobe, this turned part slips into the loop on the other end of the hoop for security.

Voilà! Who would have thought my necklace could metamorphose into such glam, New Year's Eve party–worthy earrings? Now my little spaceship really does fly me to the moon!

66   •   GET YOUR SPARKLE ON

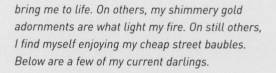

peek inside

My favorite jewels? That's a tough one. Given my jewelry obsession, it would be next to impossible for me to narrow down my most cherished gems (except for my sentimental favorites, my wedding and engagement rings, of course). Some days it is my peppy beads that bring me to life. On others, my shimmery gold adornments are what light my fire. On still others, I find myself enjoying my cheap street baubles. Below are a few of my current darlings.

One beloved piece is a coral bracelet that I made over, which originally belonged to my beautiful and crazy Nana Landis. It was broken in two places, tied in a knot, and missing several beads by the time it landed in my hands. I decided to fill the spaces left by the missing beads with small faceted brass ones. I added them close to the lovely antique clasp as a pretty detail in order to keep the coral together throughout the rest of the piece. I always picture Nana on bridge night wearing it proudly while throwing back a Harvey Wallbanger.

Two ropes of gold chain and blue Lucite beads were a major score in the Paris flea markets during a college semester abroad. The quirky '60s style and puffed disc shape of the beads in their bright blue color sang to me. Long enough to be wrapped around twice, they look perfectly adorable with blue jeans and any fun top—and are even more playful as a choker option. Best of all, I snagged them for the price of a dozen buttery croissants!

My amber beads are truly a favorite. Long before the fashion rags plastered ropes of oversized earthy, bohemian beads across their pages, my mother gave me this strand of amber honkers. I decided to convert the smaller beads into an inner strand separated by pale pink glass stones and wrap the larger ones around as a second strand in the same pattern. The result is a piece that gives a serious "Pow!" to any outfit.

smarty-pants gemstyle

SMART AND COLLEGIATE

Are you the type who knows that a diamond's sparkle is adamantine *while the glassy luster of an emerald is* vitreous—*but can't seem to remember to put on earrings unless it's a formal occasion? Can you distinguish jadeite from nephrite, but you haven't donned a string of green beads since the last millennium? Well, smarty pants, it's time to put your knowledge to practical use and add a little flair to your understated look.*

A woman with Smarty-Pants Gemstyle is probably more comfortable in a lab coat than anything with a designer label. She favors the Gap look—garments made of cotton oxford, khaki, Shetland wool, and not-too-low-cut denim. But these neutral colors and simple lines just beg for jewelry. Start by wearing our basic relaxed choker (from "Basic Necklace Assembly," page 21) in clear blue chalcedony or sweet rose quartz with a simple white T-shirt. Then explore the "Back to School Charm Bracelet" project featured in this chapter—its warm, earthy colors really perk up casual clothing. And do try the "Sassy Glasses" eyeglass chain, sure to transform any bookworm into a sexy librarian.

As you progress in your style revolution, don't be afraid to mix it up a little. I'm not suggesting you turn your closet into a rave—rather that you pair gems and outfits in unexpected ways. Don't reserve your heirloom pearls for dressing up. Throw them on with jeans and heels when you're out for a casual dinner, or try dramatic earrings with navy pants and a blazer to make the outfit more fun and less snooty. To keep those straight As coming, graduate to making your own jewelry with fascinating, esoteric stones such as smoky moldavite, or decorate yourself with green and orange fiery Mintabie opal. When the next superlatives list comes out, you'll be sure to be named "Most Dazzling."

sassy glasses

Boys do make passes at girls who wear glasses. Especially if the glasses are accented with a pretty beaded chain. Use clear crystals, or mix in colored gems. You can also try dangling charms or wire-wrapped beads to delicately fringe a length of sterling silver or gold chain. And who says it has to be small and dainty? A thick brushed gold chain could act as a funky necklace, wrapping around your lovely neck a few times while the ends clutch your glasses in front.

HOW TO

1 :: First, measure the distance from the sides of your glasses and around the back of your neck using a tape measure, and cut your wire according to where you want your glasses to fall. Attach your wire to the small, looped end of one of your eyeglass fasteners exactly as if you were attaching it to a clasp.

2 :: After closing your crimp bead, string on the beads in the following pattern: 1 silver, 5 crystal, 1 silver, 1 smoky. Repeat pattern to desired length, ending with a silver bead.

3 :: Attach your remaining eyeglass fastener with the other crimp bead. Since this chain will be handled more roughly than a necklace would, leave a bit of extra wire at the ends before closing up the crimp beads. This will give it flexibility and room for the beads to shift.

Variation: If the eyeglass chain hanging down the sides of your face annoys you, you can create the same piece, but with a large toggle clasp instead of the rubber holders. Wear the clasp in front, fold your glasses, and slip one arm of the glasses through the toggle loop.

Now, time to hit the books!

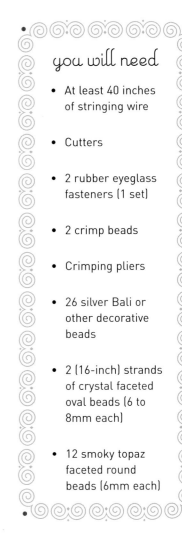

you will need

- At least 40 inches of stringing wire

- Cutters

- 2 rubber eyeglass fasteners (1 set)

- 2 crimp beads

- Crimping pliers

- 26 silver Bali or other decorative beads

- 2 (16-inch) strands of crystal faceted oval beads (6 to 8mm each)

- 12 smoky topaz faceted round beads (6mm each)

back-to-school charm bracelet

You can hear a good charm bracelet jingling from miles away. This casual, flashy number is built on an oversized, rugged gold chain meant to be as eye catching as it is tuneful. Any sturdy open-link chain will do, and you don't need to have collected a lifetime of tiny Eiffel Tower or lighthouse charms to make this fabulous bracelet. How about some delicious autumn-colored gems instead?

HOW TO

1 :: Measure your wrist using a tape measure, and cut the chain according to whether you like a lot of movement in your bracelets or prefer a more fitted feel. Don't forget to account for the length of your clasp in the fit.

2 :: Fashion the individual bead charms that will hang off the bracelet. There is no specific pattern for making or adding bead charms to this bracelet, which is what gives it its playful and all-mixed-up feeling. Stack different combinations of 2 or 3 stones on the head pins. Use a gold bead somewhere on each charm to give one element of consistency throughout the bracelet. Close the charms with your round-nose pliers, making a simple loop on each (see "Simple Loop," page 24).

3 :: Once you have made about 15 to 20 charms, play around with them and determine their final order by lining them up next to the section of chain. Space the charms evenly along the chain to avoid having gaps in your bracelet.

4 :: Use flat-nose pliers to carefully open each *charm* loop (not chain link!), slip the charm onto a link of chain, and close.

5 :: Use a jump ring to attach the clasp by opening it slightly and slipping it on both the end link of the chain and one half of the clasp. Slowly and tightly close. Repeat with the opposite side of the bracelet and clasp.

you will need

- 8 to 9 inches of gold link chain

- Cutters

- 4 or 5 each of 4 or 5 different types of drilled stones (such as golden brown carnelian, orange carnelian, yellow citrine, and a mixed assortment of gold decorative beads)

- 20 to 30 gold head pins (preferably ones with decorative ends)

- Round-nose pliers

- Flat-nose pliers

- 2 heavy gauge (strong) jump rings

- Gold toggle clasp

bright idea

ECONOMICS 101

Jewelry is jewelry, regardless of pedigree. It doesn't have to be expensive to look like a million bucks. If the fakes make you feel fab, go nuts. And remember, good things come in small packages, but they can also be found in superstores and malls! Two of my favorite cheap-but-chic sources are Kmart and Claire's Accessories. One summer day, I stumbled into the Kmart in Bridgehampton, New York, looking for tiki torches and emerged a Tahitian princess with armfuls of faux baubles—multiple-sized hoop earrings and stacks of gleaming "gold" bangles. Buying cheap jewelry is a budget-friendly way to have a fling with a fashion trend without making a lifetime commitment. If you really love an item, make sure to buy a few and store away the extras somewhere safe. For instance, silver paint on wooden beads shimmers under the summer sun but will probably chip off by the time autumn winds begin to blow, so tuck away another one for next year. It took me only a few months to rotate through three stacks of my Kmart bracelets, and I was definitely glad to have extras on hand.

Don't hesitate to use your new jewelry-making skills on your thrifty treasures. Do those glitzy beaded shoulder-duster earrings sting your delicate lobes? Grab your pliers and switch the dicey ear wire for a real gold or sterling silver one. Got a funky gobstopper pendant on a hideously cheesy gunmetal chain? Hack it off the chain and slip it onto a delicate silver one, or a soft suede cord. Better yet, add the pendant to your favorite strand of gemstones, using those wire-wrapping techniques you've been practicing!

GEMOLOGY 101

Gemstones are minerals found all over the world in concentrated areas, called deposits, below the Earth's surface. They can also be found in rocks carried by rivers or the sea. A deposit that is being "worked" is a *mine*. Mining processes vary greatly in different parts of the world; some miners still use pickaxes and baskets while others incorporate high-tech machinery. After stones are dug up, they are sent to a secondary location for processing, where they are cleaned, cut (to add facets), and polished, known as *lapidary* work. Stones that have been selected to become beads are then sent to another location for drilling. Drilling a hole through a stone is a delicate process that, much like mining, incorporates both centuries-old methods and modern procedures. Some lapidaries use handheld drills, while others employ ultrasound equipment. Once they are drilled, the gems are sold to vendors, who export them to other countries. Gemstone importers then sell the stones, often prestrung as 15-inch strands, either to designers and retailers, or directly to the general public.

So you think you're a jewelry whiz?
Test your knowledge by identifying the correct definition of each of the terms below.

1. VERMEIL
a. A hollow base metal
b. French word for "pest"
c. Gold over sterling silver
d. Translucent colored enamel

2. JUMP RING
a. A Celtic brooch with a long, hinged pin
b. A circular metal ring used to attach two links
c. The concentric color striations of malachite and agate
d. A simple silver band exchanged at a shotgun wedding

3. INTAGLIO
a. A method of hammering metal used in ancient Rome
b. Pasta with olive oil and Parmesan cheese
c. A design cut into the surface of a gemstone
d. Inlaid ivory or horn

4. CABOCHON
a. A dome-shaped stone with no facets
b. A brooch set with an emerald-cut diamond
c. A taxi for pigs
d. A precious stone weighing more than 100 karats

5. MOHS SCALE
a. A scale that measures a substance's hardness when scratched
b. An international scale that measures the value of precious stones
c. A scale that mercifully weighs 5 pounds too low
d. A scale that measures the refraction of light through crystals

6. NACRE
a. Insects, botanical matter, and other foreign substances suspended in amber
b. A dark metal alloy used for shading gold and silver
c. A crystalline substance used in the bathrooms of Studio 54
d. A crystalline substance oysters secrete that forms pearls

7. TORSADE
a. A heavily ornamented clasp
b. A necklace made of twisted strands of gems or beads
c. A Baroque jeweled shoe buckle
d. A sword used by Hobbits

8. BRIOLETTE
a. A pear-shaped cut gemstone with triangular facets
b. A pear tart with vanilla custard
c. A jeweled hat pin
d. A string of tiny seed pearls

9. FINDINGS
a. Antique jewels reworked into modern settings
b. Precious metal scraps
c. Toenail clippings on the pedicure station floor
d. Basic elements used in making jewelry

10. PARURE
a. The sensation of discomfort experienced when walking out on a really bad movie
b. A matching set of jewelry
c. The natural line where a mineral's crystal structure breaks
d. An opera-length pearl necklace

11. LAPIDARY
a. A secured storehouse for crown jewels
b. A bunny farm
c. Someone who cuts and polishes gemstones
d. Someone who sells gemstones and other minerals

12. PASTE
a. Glass cut and faceted to look like gemstones
b. Adhesive used for securing rhinestones over colored foil
c. Low-quality opals
d. Tapioca pudding served in elementary school cafeterias

Answers: 1. c; 2. b; 3. c; 4. a; 5. a; 6. d; 7. b; 8. a; 9. d; 10. b; 11. c; 12. a

bohemian gemstyle

COLORFUL AND ARTSY

FRIDA KAHLO

A woman with Bohemian Gemstyle doesn't follow the trends, though she often sets them. She is a gypsy whose disorderly jewel box is a window into her free-spirited, peripatetic soul. She may wear vintage crystal beads discovered in Prague, silver from Guatemala, ebony bracelets haggled over at an open market in Senegal. Bohemian jewels echo with memories of their place of origin or resonate with the spirit of the artisan who made them. The wearer may even be in touch with the mystical attributes of the stones. A Bohemian mixes it all up effortlessly. Layered chain and beaded necklaces, jingling armfuls of bangles, and ornate earrings work together to create a boho look that is artistic and carefree.

One of the godmothers of Bohemian Gemstyle was Frida Kahlo. She was a fierce champion of her native Mexico's handicrafts. She proudly wore vivid "ethnic" jewels and bold, intricately worked earrings decorated with traditional motifs. She adorned herself with ropes of chunky handmade beads and swaths of bright-hued loomed cloth in an era when sleek Hollywood glamour dominated the fashion scene. Many of her self-portraits feature jewelry as an important visual element and also one coded with symbolism—as seen in a dangling earring shaped as a hand, or a necklace strung with bone fragments.

To translate this look to your own jewelry wardrobe, seek out baubles with natural textures and organic shapes. Choose natural, earthy tones like the warm browns of carnelians or the rusty red of garnets over primary brights. Experiment with silver if you usually wear gold, or try the subtle, mysterious glow of moonstone as a change from the luster of pearls. Tiger's eye, a mellow yellow-brown stone with a flash of fire, is a classic bohemian choice.

For a more streamlined take on Bohemian Gemstyle, simple, unfussy settings can look prettily artsy and unpretentious: a black silk or chocolate leather cord can highlight the chunky irregularity of piercing blue turquoise or honeyed, golden amber nuggets, for example. Just remember: to keep from looking like a cyclone hit you at a Grateful Dead concert, try wearing only a few pieces at one time.

chunky monkey choker

Chunky, heavy stones are not just for gypsy queens (or Wilma and Betty). Today's sleekest runway looks pair oversized, earthy baubles with the haute-est of fashion frocks. Taking a cue from the designers, wear one jumbo necklace as a focal point with minimalist clothing, or add it to the eclectic layers and accoutrements of a boho outfit.

No longer limited to cowgirl and Southwestern styles, turquoise has galloped into mainstream fashion over the past decade. Turquoise and silver are a natural combination, because traditional Native American jewelry often mixes the two. But why not depart from tradition and pair your blue-sky rocks with a touch of sunlit gold? To make this piece, use the "Basic Necklace Assembly" technique.

HOW TO

1 :: If your stones are graduated in size, start stringing from the center using the largest stone, and add from alternating sides with each successive smaller stone. Alternate stones with gold round beads and bead caps.

2 :: Use a heavy clasp and a double set of crimps on each side to attach the clasp, and follow the steps for "Basic Necklace Assembly," page 21.

you will need

- 20 inches of heavy wire (.019 gauge or higher)

- 16 inches' worth of chunky turquoise nuggets

- Small round gold beads

- Gold domed bead caps (used on the sides of each stone for decorative detail)

- Heavy clasp

- Crimp beads

- Crimping pliers

- Cutters

knock-on-wood bracelet

Underscoring the hip in hippie, the wood beads in this easy bracelet look chic when accented with coral, bone, gold, and agate. Stacked or worn solo, it can go upscale when paired with cream or camel clothing or casual with a denim mini.

HOW TO

1 :: Measure your wrist using a tape measure, and cut a length of Invisiline that is 2 to 3 inches longer than needed to go around your wrist.

2 :: After deciding on your bead pattern, attach a piece of tape to one end of the Invisiline, and begin stringing on your beads from the other side. (Determining the length of beads can be challenging with elastic because of its stretch. You will want to stop adding beads when you have enough to wrap around your wrist comfortably *without* having to pull or stretch out the elastic.)

3 :: Once your beads have reached the correct length, remove the tape. Pinch both ends of remaining elastic together where they meet, and slip your arm out. Holding that spot, wrap the ends of both strands of elastic around your thumb and push them through the loop, making a knot. Tighten gently but firmly.

4 :: Carefully place a dab of glue directly onto the knot. Let it dry for about 20 minutes. After the glue is dry, trim the excess elastic, leaving about 2mm sticking out. Hide the knot inside one of the beads.

you will need

- 10 inches of Invisiline or Stretch Magic (clear elastic cord)

- 8 inches' worth of beads (carved wood, bone, cork, coral, and gold in mixed sizes)

- Craft or jeweler's glue

bewitched, bothered, and bejeweled

Having a Stevie Nicks moment and feeling witchy? Or maybe you're just out of sorts (and possibly a tad bitchy). Finish up that chicken soup, get out of bed, and make your best rocks perform double duty. The healing properties of gemstones have been recorded for centuries, but stone therapy probably began far earlier, deep in prehistoric times. Some scholars and folklorists speculate that humans may have started wearing jewelry not just because of its looks but also because of the talismanic powers ascribed to certain gems. Birthstones, for example, were first worn as amulets.

Today, healers use stones to cure many ailments, both physical and psychic, using a system of correspondences dating back to before the Middle Ages. Some practitioners believe that stones absorb energy from the sun, the moon, and the heat of their own formation, and that this energy can be released and unblocks trapped chi (vital forces) in the human body. To tap into a stone's powers you can lay it on the chakra, or energy center, that it relates to or simply wear it as jewelry. Faster than you can say "Ohm," it will work its special magic. Now you'll know to don your carnelians to secure that second date!

gemstone correspondences

CHAKRA • COLOR	BODY	MIND/SPIRIT	STONE
FIRST • RED	BASE OF SPINE	VITALITY, SURVIVAL	GARNET, SMOKY QUARTZ, OBSIDIAN
SECOND • ORANGE	BELLY	DESIRE, SEXUALITY	CARNELIAN, TIGER'S EYE
THIRD • YELLOW	SOLAR PLEXUS	EGO	CITRINE, YELLOW CALCITE
FOURTH • GREEN, PINK	HEART	COMPASSION	ROSE QUARTZ, KUNZITE, ADVENTURINE, WATERMELON TOURMALINE
FIFTH • LIGHT BLUE	THROAT	COMMUNICATION, CREATIVITY	AQUAMARINE, AZURITE SODALITE
SIXTH • INDIGO	FOREHEAD	PSYCHIC SIGHT	LAPIS, CLEAR QUARTZ
SEVENTH • VIOLET	CROWN OF HEAD	SPIRITUALITY, ONENESS	AMETHYST, OPAL

Some properties attributed to other popular gemstones include the following:

Agate: Strength, energy

Bloodstone: Soothing

Coral: Protection at sea

Emerald: Foresight, heightened psychic receptivity

Garnet: Physical strength, wisdom

Hematite: Courage

Jade: Protection from harm, inner beauty

Moonstone: Long life and friendship

Onyx: Devotion and concentration, repulsion of negativity

Pearl: Protection, intuition

Peridot: Compassion, delight in simple pleasure

Ruby: Attraction of deep love

Sapphire: Peace of mind, good fortune

Topaz: Courage, warmth

Turquoise: Physical protection if bestowed as a gift

birthstones

ARIES
MARCH 21–APRIL 20

DIAMOND

LEO
JULY 23–AUGUST 23

PERIDOT

SAGITTARIUS
NOVEMBER 23–DECEMBER 21

TURQUOISE, ZIRCON

TAURUS
APRIL 21–MAY 21

EMERALD

VIRGO
AUGUST 24–SEPTEMBER 23

SAPPHIRE

CAPRICORN
DECEMBER 22–JANUARY 20

GARNET

GEMINI
MAY 22–JUNE 21

PEARL, MOONSTONE,
ALEXANDRITE

LIBRA
SEPTEMBER 24–OCTOBER 23

OPAL, TOURMALINE

AQUARIUS
JANUARY 21–FEBRUARY 19

AMETHYST

CANCER
JUNE 22–JULY 22

RUBY

SCORPIO
OCTOBER 24–NOVEMBER 22

TOPAZ, CITRINE

PISCES
FEBRUARY 20–MARCH 20

AQUAMARINE,
BLOODSTONE

how bedazzling

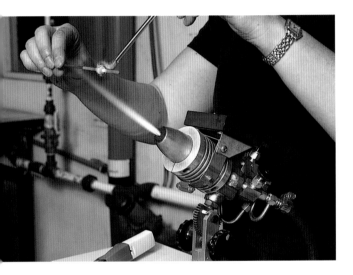

One-of-a-kind handmade glass beads are gorgeous and make a striking accent when added to stones. Since glass comes in more hues than Baskin-Robbins has flavors, the color possibilities are endless. Traditionally, glass beads were made by heating the materials over an oil lamp, hence the term for making beads: "lamp working." To make a bead today, artisans wrap molten glass around a mandrel (a metal rod that determines what size the hole will be). In 1997, the first artist-access glass-working studio in the United States, Urban Glass of Brooklyn, New York, founded a program called the Bead Project, which awards scholarships to low-income women so they can learn how to make glass beads and fashion them into high-style jewelry as a career. Now that's what I call getting your sparkle on!

executive gemstyle

POLISHED AND PROFESSIONAL

Today's professional women have worked hard to earn their colors, be they garnet red, lemon quartz yellow, or peridot green. While the classic workday pearl choker will never be out of style, staid, fuddy-duddy jewels have gone the way of sneakers worn with pantyhose. Today's softer, fitted executive styles call for more interesting jewels—proving professional does not equal boring. Delicate links of silver and gold chain with finely crafted pendants complement an executive look without overpowering it. Clear purple amethyst and true blue lapis are also clean, classic color choices. If your workplace is on the conservative side, snazz up your traditional suits with a rich-colored gemstone necklace like the one featured in this chapter. A bold Art Deco brooch or a gleaming ring set with some serious rocks can also make quieter clothing sing. Looking for an unexpected dash of color? Try watermelon tourmaline or milky jade. According to stone lore, these green gems stimulate wisdom and intelligence—just what you need to get through the work week!

For an eye-catching variation on that everyday pearl necklace, follow the lead of Avon's CEO, Andrea Jung, who has made a decadent three-strand choker her signature piece. Rarely is she spotted without it. Mattel even created a Barbie doll in her image—pearls and all. If they seem a little matronly for you, try color-dipped freshwater pearls. Ranging from pale pinks and buttery yellows to majestic peacock blues and purples, these iridescent little treasures can be relied on to perk up neutral fabrics quicker than you can say "Get me the ETA on those stats ASAP!" Luxurious Tahitian black pearls exude grown-up glamour and sophistication without crossing any lines of propriety. And if you super-size any of these jewels, they will whisk you out of the office and straight into happy hour!

ALL JAZZED UP
Here's a little cheat sheet for mixing fabrics and jewels:

- Enliven neutral camel with a burst of turquoise.

- Pinstripes shouldn't make you feel imprisoned—try a splash of red-orange coral, particularly in the fall when warmer tones come back into season.

- Complement yummy tweeds and flannels with smoky colors like topaz and labradorite, or lighten up these woolly fabrics with creamy peach moonstones.

- Even if you work in a creative environment where denim is de rigueur, nothing makes those jeans more office appropriate than a luxurious strand of marble-sized crystal quartz.

POP ROCKS
We asked Teril Turner, director of marketing and publicity at Henri Bendel, to comment on her favorite jewelry styles for work:

"Because I work in the fashion industry, I have a little more freedom than many women in what I am able to wear to the office. Still, I try to convey a professional, pulled-together look, and a few select pieces of jewelry make this easy.

"Eye-catching jewels, such as a one-of-a-kind pendant or bold cuff set with gemstones, are a fabulous way to add a touch of individuality to a tailored suit or a pop of color to an all-black look. A variation on this formula is to layer black jewelry over a monochrome black outfit. This creates depth and dimension through varied textures and materials such as a black jet necklace paired with a black leather cuff trimmed in ribbon or charms. Though I would not wear vintage clothing to work, an office wardrobe can be the perfect foil for a unique piece of vintage jewelry.

"I look for simple, strong pieces and avoid anything fussy. My jewelry wardrobe revolves around a few basics, which I almost never take off: a Cartier tank watch, diamond stud earrings, and my platinum wedding ring. To bring an outfit to life, I often layer on one or two more key pieces, often in white or colored stones."

rock, scissors, paperweight

Give your desk a mini makeover and add some sparkle to your work space. After all, you spend enough time there. And you just might get through that pile of papers more quickly if they're tidied up with a big, glamorous jewel. This paperweight also makes a nice gift when you need to kiss up to the boss! I used smoky topaz, but you can use any large, gorgeous stone.

HOW TO

1 :: Start by examining your stone to find its flattest side. Roll it around on a flat surface and determine exactly where it sits most naturally. This spot will become its permanent bottom.

2 :: Using shears, cut a piece of felt to glue on bottom. It doesn't matter if it's round or irregular, as long as you can't see it underneath the stone when viewing it from the side.

3 :: Place a few drops of glue on the bottom of the stone and also on the felt, and press together. Leave the stone upside down to dry for at least 20 minutes.

you will need

- 1 large, heavy, beautiful faceted stone (no drill hole required)

- Sewing shears or sharp scissors

- 2- to 3-inch square of colored felt to match your stone

- Craft or jeweler's glue

odd-bead-out necklace

Soften the lines of your work wardrobe with one gorgeous off-center bead. This necklace is loaded with personality but sophisticated enough to go with crisp shirts and smart suits. Select a strand of gemstones as the base of the necklace, and then one individual stone, preferably equal to or slightly larger than the others, as your focal point. For this sophisticated necklace, I used beautiful large, faceted lemon topaz nuggets and one carved, barrel-shaped, antiqued gold bead. In making this project, you'll use the skills you learned making the "Basic Necklace."

HOW TO

1 :: Follow the steps for beginning the "Basic Necklace Assembly," page 21.

2 :: When stringing the stones onto your wire, add the focal point bead in the position *two* places over from the center, either left or right. Placing it *one* spot from the center might look accidental, but positioning it two spots over will affirm its intentional location and playful, off-center spirit.

Tip: If the stones you choose for this or any necklace are particularly angular and cause the wire to be exposed at a curving point in the piece, try inserting a tiny (1mm) seed bead in a color similar to the adjacent stones. This subtle addition helps achieve a more professional look.

Clasps can be as decorative as the jewels they hold together. Turn a beautifully clasped necklace around to the front for a different look. Toggle clasps also make good eyeglass holders.

peek inside

Here's what Teril had to say about the contents of her jewel box:

"I rarely wear these garnet cluster earrings and necklace [by Trish Becker] as a set, because garnets mix so well with other pieces. The strong red color is dramatic but surprisingly neutral. Garnet happens to be my birthstone, and the moment I laid eyes on these pieces at a charity auction, I knew they were destined for my jewelry box.

"My double strand chalcedony necklace is one of my favorites because a dear friend designed it for me at Femmegems as a gift to celebrate the completion of my master's degree. The serene, waterlike quality of the stones is a visual antidote to the craziness of my life.

"I treated myself to this irresistible Alex Woo topaz cocktail ring because it was, well, irresistible! Every woman needs at least one knockout ring and the bold yet simple style of this wonderful indulgence really struck me.

"Designer Lulu Frost reinvents vintage elements into timeless jewels. This pendant was originally a Victorian shoe buckle. The grasshopper reminds me of an Egyptian scarab or funky spider pin because it appears elegant and ladylike at first glance but is still a little subversive. I love the sense of history, drama, and unexpected humor it represents."

beach babe gemstyle

LAID-BACK & HIP

BO DEREK

You may not remember the plot of the movie 10, but who can forget Bo Derek running across the sand with her halo of beaded braids? Her lost-on-a-desert-island look forever transformed beach style from "Gidget" to "Goddess."

Hot, salty, sandy days call for clothing and jewelry with a relaxed but decidedly sexy vibe. Vacation is the perfect time to experiment with jewels you would never wear to work—huge hoops, a dainty toe ring, or, for those with the firmest abs, a delicate belly chain. Faded, sea-washed colors tend to reflect nature while candy brights and black and white look fresh and elegant even in wilting heat. Beachy gems, like those in the glamorous necklace featured in this chapter, can be plucked straight from the sea: mother-of-pearl, coral, and shells. Minimalist jewelry, like our "Catch-a-Wave Choker" on page 100 (a great gift for the cabana boy in your life) or necklaces and bracelets fashioned from rope and mother-of-pearl chunks, capture the simplicity of Beach Babe Gemstyle. Cool, watery colors look fluid and easy, from swimming-pool blue to stormier ocean tones. Try a mixture of blue lace agates and amazonites to achieve an affordable blend of hushed blue-greens, or a combination of blue topaz and aquamarines for a trendier marine hue.

Balmy summer nights call for an entirely different look. A mixture of apatite, black coral, and the smoky gray-blue-green flicker of labradorite look cool in the moonlight on a steamy evening. Going to a pool party? Why not try super-short shorts and iridescent moonstones to show off that tan? Combine the moonstones with mother-of-pearl and tiny baroque pearls to create a sensuous neckline collage of soft, slinky, shimmery whites. And don't be afraid to pull out some status jewelry when you are lounging beachside, day or night. Thick gold and silver chains and glittering gemstones sizzle both in the bright sunshine and under the twinkling stars.

she sells seashells necklace

Beach jewelry does not mean just puka shells and braided rope bracelets. This summer, why don't you gussy up those cute tanks and flip-flops with this luscious beach-goddess number instead? Or toss it on with a skimpy white dress and a little bronzer for a sunset beach party! The length of the branch coral pieces makes this a fairly substantial necklace, so it is better worn long than as a choker. Don't be daunted by the irregular shape of branch coral pieces—they behave just like beads.

HOW TO

1 :: If the branch coral pieces are graduated in size, lay out your pattern in such a way that an equal number of pieces on each side radiate from the center shell from longest to shortest. Save 3 of the longest and most uniquely shaped pieces to hang behind the shell.

2 :: Using your round-nose pliers and gold head pins, wire wrap a loop onto the top of each of the 3 reserved coral pieces.

3 :: Measure and cut the 3 sections of chain that will hang slightly unevenly from the back of the shell. Each should dangle about one-half to one-quarter inch below the edge of the shell.

4 :: Connect each section of chain to the loops of the wire-wrapped coral pieces with a jump ring (see illustration, page 96).

5 :: Join all 3 pieces of chain at their tops with the remaining jump ring and string it onto your necklace wire (see illustration, page 96).

6 :: After adding your dangling branches, string on clear beads to each side of the jump ring until they fill out the space underneath the shell (which will rest over the chains). Adding these small beads will anchor and center the

- 16- to 18-inch strand of branch coral pieces (drilled like beads)

- Round-nose pliers

- 3 thin gold head pins

- 12 inches of small gold link chain

- Cutters

- 4 gold jump rings

- 24 inches of wire

- Approximately 15 clear small beads (3–4mm)

- 1 medium to large seashell, real or faux (drilled on the left and right sides)

- Heavy gold clasp

- 4 crimp beads

- Flat-nose or crimping pliers (depending on preferred crimping method)

chains and keep them from sliding back and forth from one side of the shell to the other (see illustration).

7 :: Once you have strung on your shell and successfully centered the chains beneath it with smaller beads, you can begin to add the branches in descending order from each side of the shell. Don't worry if they don't sit perfectly straight or flat, this is the natural, irregular beauty of coral.

8 :: To finish, add a clasp to the top of the necklace using your preferred crimping method.

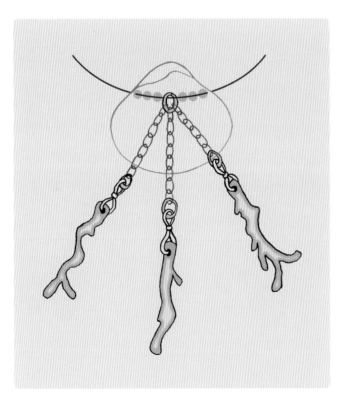

Variation: If you cannot find a shell pendant that is drilled on both sides, you can utilize one that is drilled with a single center hole. Using a head pin to wire wrap a loop through its top, you can then string the shell directly onto the necklace wire as a pendant. The dangling coral chain pieces can be added to the left and right sides of the shell and hang down behind or in front of it.

Tip: If you have some extra pieces of branch coral left over, you can wire wrap yourself into a swinging-coral-earring mania and give them to your most fabulous friends as holiday gifts!

bright idea

TOO DARN HOT

Think bikinis and bijoux don't mix? Think again. Summertime jewels needn't end at the ears, wrist, or throat. Sarongs, flip-flops, hair bands and clips, beach bags, and even swimsuits can all be adorned with gemstones and beads. Use colorless multipurpose craft glue to bejewel a barrette. Or attach vintage clip-on earrings to the top of your thong sandals for added color and pizzazz. Balance and proportion are key: if your crocheted bikini bottoms feature dangling puka shells, then skip the layered gold chains. Similarly, if your one-piece suit is a glam, gold-bedecked number, then leave your jingling, jangling gypsy sarong in the cabana. So how do yummy mummies accessorize a sleek black two-piece or minimalist maillot while watching over their little chicks by the shore? Huge sunglasses and a fat Tiffany silver chain, naturally. See? Finding *your* inner hot mama is a (sea) breeze.

two-of-a-kind anklets

Remember the adorable Mother's Day macaroni necklace your little one made in kindergarten? Of course you do—it's still proudly displayed on your bureau. Help her to update her skills with a sweet, beachy mother-daughter anklet project. Or try this one with a friend.

HOW TO

1 :: Measure your ankles using a tape measure. A typical adult anklet length is 9 inches; a child's anklet will range in size depending on age.

2 :: Add one half of your clasp (the lobster claw) to the end of your wire for each anklet using a crimp bead (see "Adding a Clasp: The Fold-Over Crimping Method," page 23).

3 :: Lay out two sets of matching patterns of beads, with an inch or two extra for Mom's anklet. String beads onto the respective wires.

4 :: Once the lengths are completed, attach the other half of the clasps and the soldered jump rings to the wire ends with crimp beads.

5 :: Mom may want to help attach the charms to both anklets: Using flat-nose pliers, gently open the remaining jump ring and slip it through the charm. Then loop it through the soldered jump ring that hooks into the lobster claw to finish the anklet. Close up gently but firmly with flat-nose pliers. Repeat for second anklet.

you will need

- 2 silver lobster claw clasps and attaching *soldered* jump rings

- Approximately 22 inches of thin wire

- 4 silver crimp beads

- Crimping pliers

- Cutters

- Approximately 20 inches' worth of assorted light-blue and-green beads

- 2 matching beach-inspired charms

- 2 *nonsoldered* jump rings

- Flat-nose pliers

catch-a-wave choker

Here is something for your very own surfer boy (or surfer boy at heart). The coil clasps in this project can also be used with thick silk or suede cord and a smooth piece of jade to make a pretty, Zen-inspired choker.

HOW TO

1 :: Measure out the desired length of cord, and cut it 1 inch shorter (length will be made up with coil clasps and lobster claw).

2 :: String selected bead onto cord. (If the drill hole is not large enough to accommodate the cord, you can wire wrap it and transform it into a dangling pendant.)

3 :: Add a bit of glue to the end of the cord and immediately slip on a coil clasp, pushing it all the way down onto the end of the cord. Using your flat-nose pliers, squeeze down and slowly pinch the outer ring of the coil until it firmly grabs the cord (see illustration). Repeat on other side. Let glue dry for 20 minutes before you test with a firm tug.

4 :: Use your round-nose pliers to smooth out any protruding pieces of metal on the coil. To finish, connect the coil clasp to the lobster claw clasp with jump rings.

Surf's up. Hang ten!

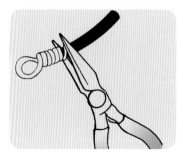

you will need

- Approximately 22 inches of leather cord in any color

- 1 large wood bead (or shell or pendant)

- Craft or jeweler's glue

- 2 coil clasps

- Flat-nose pliers

- Round-nose pliers

- Lobster claw clasp

- 2 jump rings

rock star gemstyle

EDGY AND FUN

Whether you wear door-knocker earrings or an armful of black rubber bracelets, a girl with Rock Star Gemstyle takes her cues from the street. It's all about mixing hard and soft, tough and vulnerable, for rebellious and in-your-face fashion that hides a "heart of glass" (remember Blondie?).

If you are into *heavy metal*, think buckles, grommets, heavy-duty zippers, and thick linked chains. Make them girly by adding the sparkle of crystal: try our "Flea Market Makeover" necklace (page 104), which pairs chain with scavenged orange chandelier drops. Dark, industrial colors also play up the gritty, night-owl feel of rock 'n' roll gems. Match brushed stainless steel, gunmetal, or oxidized silver with the oil-slick sheen of marcasite or hematite gemstones. Do you love the bad-girl vibe but aren't quite ready to go full-on ghetto fabulous or down-and-dirty grunge? Toss on one key piece—a ropy gold chain with a cheeky medallion or a punky studded bracelet, for example—and don a buttery-soft leather motorcycle jacket and stiletto boots.

If you are feeling a little more Joss Stone than Joan Jett, try baubles with an antique look. These jewels can have a distinct Rock Star Gemstyle, especially black mourning jewelry from the early Victorian period, and ornate, iron pieces from the Gothic Revival of the eighteenth and nineteenth centuries (think '80s Madonna with her piled-on crosses). Inky, polished jet jewels like those worn by Queen Victoria can create a mysterious, *goth* style. To achieve this look yourself, try using garnets, bloodstone, or onyx mixed with sterling silver charms and pendants.

Going for a slightly softer style? Take these pieces down in size and layer them for a "rich hippie" look. Add feather earrings, big hoops loaded with tiny gemstone beads, or shoulder dusters like the ones that follow for a style that travels easily from a sunny afternoon at a music festival to a sultry dinner at a sleek downtown hot spot. Show some skin with a sexy halter and low-slung Indian print skirt, and stack on silver rings and bangles. Haven't used that second (or third) ear piercing since you were sixteen? Now is the time to add a tiny hoop or two to your usual danglies. Spread your wings, iron butterfly.

secret agent man

THE ROCKS THAT YOU GOT

Rocker chick that you are, I know you're at least a little subversive. So why not subtly (okay, shamelessly) hint at what you'd like for your next special-occasion gift? Give the man in your life another use for his pliers by slyly leaving this section open on his bedside table.

Recently, Mason, handsome rocker boyfriend of Sacha, a favorite Femmegems customer, asked us to take him on a makeover expedition for a very special purpose: to make something personal and original for her birthday. Knowing that her taste is more downtown edge than uptown ruffle and that she loves thrift-store shopping, we set our sights on New York City's Chelsea Flea Market for a one-of-a-kind design session.

Together, Mason and I pored over the endless tables of trash and treasures and gathered elements that we could transform into a perfect and personalized gift. The winners of the day: a white chain necklace with an oversized mesh pendant, an antique amethyst and gold ring, a tarnished gold locket, three orange glass crystals from a chandelier, a small, old-fashioned key, a small heart charm with a tiny rhinestone, a faceted glass disco-ball-style earring, and a distressed wide-link gold chain.

Back at the store, and using "charm bracelet meets the Lower East Side" as our mantra, we played with a variety of options, sketched a few, and settled on the look of the final piece.

flea market makeover jewels

HOW TO

1 ∷ We attached the unusual white pendant to the gold chain using jump rings.

2 ∷ A 3-inch section of the white chain was cut and then attached, just above the center of the gold chain on each side, using jump rings. Before attaching the second side, we slipped the gold ring onto the chain so that it would dangle.

3 ∷ An inch above that connection on the right side, we attached the locket, about which Mason joked that Sacha could perhaps use it to hold a picture of someone special.

4 ∷ About an inch and a half above the connection on the left side, we lined up our three charms—the key, heart, and disco ball—and attached them using more jump rings and some wire wrapping.

5 ∷ Having gotten to this point with the necklace, we had the 3 chandelier crystals left over. We decided that 2 would make perfectly fabulous rocker earrings and the remaining crystal would pull it together as an ensemble if we included them in the necklace somehow. "Well, she loves big funky pendants," Mason remarked, and with that, we wire wrapped all 3 crystals, attached 2 of them to gold ear wires for earrings, and cast the remaining one dangling off the mesh pendant.

With a little imagination, some manly deconstruction, and a few jump rings, you can come up your own one-of-a-kind flea market couture. Your special gal will be truly grateful. Just ask Mason.

shoulder-duster earrings

Small, demure earrings can be sweet by day, but shoulder dusters dare you to walk on the wild side at night. They draw attention to a bare neck and shoulders while looking fabulous swinging on the dance floor. These earrings are made by attaching five sections of looped head pins, each stacked with black and gold beads, which allows for sexy shimmy throughout the length of the earring.

HOW TO

1 :: Using your round-nose pliers, make simple loops on the end of each head pin except for 2 head pins (see "Simple Loop," page 24).

2 :: Using cutters, cut the top (the "head" of the pin) off all pins except the 2 without the simple loops so that you can slide beads onto them.

3 :: Stack a section of beads onto each pin following the patterns below. The last section (E) will be the bottom section of the earring, so you'll use the pins with the untrimmed heads for these. Each pin will act as a section connecting via the loops you've created on the pins. Following are the sectioned patterns A through E (from bottom to top):

> **A:** 3 brass, 1 black round, 7 brass
> **B:** 1 black round, 1 brass round, 1 blank rondel, 1 gold
> **C:** 1 brass, 1 black round, 1 black rondel, 1 brass
> **D:** 1 brass, 1 black round, 1 black rondel, 1 gold
> **E:** 1 brass, 1 black large

4 :: To attach each section, work from bottom to top. After you have stacked each section of beads onto each pin, create a loop over the top bead. Attach section A to the bottom loop of your ear wire, making it the earring's first hanging component.

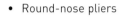

you will need

- Round-nose pliers

- 10 gold head pins

- Cutters

- 30 small faceted brass beads (2 to 3mm each)

- 8 small round faceted black beads (4mm each)

- 6 donut-shaped black rondel beads (6mm each)

- 4 corrugated gold beads (6mm each)

- 1 pair gold ear wires

5 :: Attach each additional lettered section, in order, to the piece above it, using the same method of making simple loops atop each open pin. The last section (E) has the untrimmed head remaining on its bottom anchoring the whole earring.

6 :: Repeat steps 3 through 5 to make the matching earring.

Variations: These earrings can be made in a million different ways—longer, shorter, and with endless varieties of beads and stones—using this basic technique. You can also experiment by attaching sections of beads to hoops or posts for a different style, or using a single dangling stone in place of an entire section.

THE GOOD, THE BAD, AND THE UGLY

Wearing Vintage Jewelry

Vintage pieces can range from the wild and wacky to the traditional, from works of art to lovely junk. Whether you find your baubles at a posh antiques store or the Salvation Army, high-quality vintage jewelry represents the style of a certain era. Lots of jewelry is old, but vintage *implies its notable design and secures its place in fashion history.*

Some of the best vintage pieces are highly collectible costume jewels from the 1920s through the 1950s (and earlier). The term *costume jewelry* was coined in the 1920s to refer to items that were beautiful but lacking the monetary value of precious materials. However, the craftsmanship of many of these older pieces can be exquisite and sometimes rivals that of fine jewelry. Because of this attention to detail, good vintage jewelry can be pricey. When purchasing vintage jewelry of any value, inspect it carefully. The previous owner might have been a grande dame who polished and cradled her gems with great care, or a sassy exhibitionist who used them as contraptions to hold up her pole-dancing gear.

A keen eye can still find fun old gems in junk shops, flea markets, and tag sales (and Granny's jewel box). However, it can be a challenge to wear thrift store pieces without looking like you're wearing pieces from, well...a thrift store. Find a string of love beads from the 1960s tucked beneath some old quilts at a tag sale? Go for it—but wear them with your contemporary clothing. Remember, wearing vintage does not mean you have to be decked in it from head to toe. (You don't want to look like a cast member in a revival of the musical *Hair*.) But if you think you can confidently sport a total vintage look, then pile it on. To channel an '80s glamazon, how about the modern, organic shapes of jewelry designers like Robert Lee Morris and Elsa Peretti adorning the wide-shouldered power fashions of Norma Kamali or early Donna Karan?

Although you can often find new reproductions of popular vintage styles, one of the most wonderful things about authentic vintage pieces is their personal, sentimental value. Maybe it was someone's favorite, a gift from a beloved or a special hand-me-down. The mystery of this jewelry's past makes it particularly fascinating. Each piece has a story to tell, and you, by cherishing it, get to become a part of that story.

rock chick

CHICK CHAT WITH ROCKER MUFFY NIXON

We met up with rocker Muffy Nixon (dubbed a "punk princess" by W magazine) at a café in downtown New York City, where she was on tour performing songs from her debut album, Freakshow.

LINDSAY: Muffy, what's your day job?
MUFFY: Rock 'n' roll.

LINDSAY: Night job?
MUFFY: Rock 'n' roll.

LINDSAY: Dream job?
MUFFY: Guess.

LINDSAY: What do you consider to be "rock star" style?
MUFFY: I think it's all about making your own statement. Combining clothes, accessories, jewelry, hair, makeup—all of it—in a way that uniquely expresses something new and interesting is very rock 'n' roll.

LINDSAY: Who inspires you?
MUFFY: Edie Sedgwick for her total simplicity: black tights, short skirt, long earrings, and those eyes! David Bowie: glam, glam, glam. Stardust, pantsuits, the genius, best-dressed human ever!!

LINDSAY: Describe some of your favorite jewels.
MUFFY: I love super-long earrings that aren't necessarily chandeliers. I'm also obsessed with bracelets. My mom has this amazing bangle with a bit o' bling that looks like maybe twenty-five chains wound together. I had to steal it from her. When she caught me wearing it, she told me it is worn on your upper arm so you can walk like an Egyptian. On the other end of the spectrum, I love the jewelry you can buy on the street in Mexico—wooden bracelets and piles of cool silver stuff.

LINDSAY: Any dos and don'ts?
MUFFY: Only be yourself. And too much is *never* too much, especially when it comes to wearing black, eyeliner, and bangles.

park avenue gemstyle

SOPHISTICATED AND LUXE

JACKIE O.

The Park Avenue lady does not shy from adornment; in fact, she wears her "crown jewels" at breakfast, lunch, and dinner. Whether attending a charity gala or yachting in Newport, the Park Avenue lady knows just the right jewelry to complement her couture ensembles. Although her collection of important pieces might rival the windows of Van Cleef & Arpel's, she is not opposed to wearing baubles of lesser provenance. In fact, she mixes real and fake with the supreme confidence of a woman who has arrived.

Jackie O. epitomized this posh look all her life, from her days as a sporty "girl photographer" to her term as First Lady to her years as the jet-set wife of a Greek shipping magnate. During her time in the White House, Jackie's sophistication and elegance made her *the* style icon of that hopeful era. She blended European chic with American verve and carried it off with the poise of a born-and-bred Park Avenue princess.

To pull off this style, you must first embrace opulence. Forget one strand of pearls. How about a lavish torsade of six, like the "French Knot Necklace" featured in this chapter (page 112)? To mimic the look of pricey gemstones without suffering the sticker shock, dare to substitute crystal for diamonds, aventurines or jade for emeralds, ruby quartz for rubies, and lapis lazuli for sapphires. A Park Avenue lady would. As a gem connoisseur, she can distinguish a Brazilian Paraiba tourmaline from an African one, but her jewelry box (or walk-in safe) is likely to house an equal number of bold, fun costume pieces as well. In the spirit of art dealer and heiress Peggy Guggenheim, who wore eccentric, avant-garde jewelry, try our witty and luxurious "Razzle-Dazzle Tassel Earrings" (page 114).

For Park Avenue style on a budget, try a choker of gumball-sized cut glass beads in pink, coral, or orange—these brighten an elegantly cut neckline with playful assurance. Jumbo gold and silver beads look super luxe but are less expensive than precious stones. Upscale neutrals with a decadent, sensual feel include smoky topaz, faux tortoiseshell, and faux ivory. You don't need to dip into the rent money for your downtown digs to look like an uptown girl.

french knot necklace

There are no clasps on this decadent lariat. Instead, we utilize the French knot "tuck through" style of wearing a scarf, or in this case, multiple scarves.

HOW TO

1 :: To begin, cut approximately 5 feet of wire to make your first strand. Crimps will be used to secure each end of the wire and a small gold bead will act as the end piece.

2 :: Add a crimp bead to the end of one strand, followed by a small gold bead. Without closing the crimp, slip the end of the wire around the gold bead and go back through the crimp bead (as if you were attaching it to a clasp). The wire should wrap tightly around the gold bead, which you want to push flush up against the crimp bead. Using flat-nose pliers, flatten the crimp tightly and trim the remaining tip of wire.

3 :: Begin stringing on between 3 and 4 strands of pearls, occasionally adding a garnet stone (try every 3, 6, or 9 pearls—whatever pattern pleases your eye). Add more garnets to the beginning and end of the strand, as they will hang more visibly in front.

4 :: Close the opposite end using the technique described in step 1, with a crimp bead to secure a gold bead on the end.

5 :: Repeat steps 1 through 3 for the remaining 5 lariat strands, making each slightly different in length by 1 to 2 inches and subtly varying the garnet pattern near the ends.

6 :: To wear, lay all of your strands out in front of you from left to right. With one hand, grab all 6 from the middle. Holding them in front of your chest, wrap the strands around your neck so there's a loop hanging on one side and all the loose ends hanging on the other side. Pull or tuck the loose strand ends through the loop. Adjust to make a tighter loop closer to the throat or a looser one worn farther down the chest like a scarf.

you will need

- Approximately 32 feet of stringing wire
- Cutters
- 12 gold crimp beads
- Approximately 40 small gold beads
- Flat-nose pliers
- 24 (16-inch) strands of white "biwa" stick pearls
- 6 to 8 inches of small garnet rondels (2 to 3mm)

razzle-dazzle tassel earrings

Rip the tassels from your overstuffed Palm Beach couch (or visit your local trimmings store) to make these luxe, kicky earrings. The technique is simple, but the color possibilities are as endless as a Park Avenue princess's credit limit.

HOW TO

make a triangle

wrap snugly and trim,
then add a bead

bend wire 90 degrees,
then form loop in
opposite direction

1 :: If your tassel comes with a string loop for hanging on the top, start by cutting this off. Cut very close to the knotted top of the tassel without cutting *into* it, in order to avoid fraying.

2 :: Using a head pin, delicately poke the side of the knotted top of the tassel in different places until it slides through horizontally with ease. Push through until about a third of the pin is poking out the opposite side.

3 :: Using your round-nose pliers, bend both sides upward past 90 degrees until they cross over each other, making an X or a triangle over the knotted top of the tassel.

4 :: Using the technique to make a wire-wrapped loop (see "Wrapped Loop," page 25), use your flat-nose pliers to wrap one side of the crossed head pin around the opposite side. This will become the connector between the tassel and your earring finding.

5 :: Trim excess wire, and center the opposite remaining section of the head pin by bending it upward slightly.

6 :: Slide the decorative gold bead over the top of the remaining section of head pin. Finish by making a simple loop over that bead and hooking on your earring posts or ear wires before closing the loop using your flat-nose pliers.

7 :: Repeat the steps above to make the matching tassel earring.

TWIST AND SHOUT

A simple strand of beads can look lovely and minimalist, but when you want to wear an opulent wreath of jewels, try twisting together a few of your favorite necklaces to make a multistrand torsade. Note that irregular shapes "grab" each other with more ease than even, polished stones, as seen in this necklace.

HOW TO

1 :: Start by holding all the necklace ends together in your left hand.

2 :: With your right hand, grab all the strands and, while keeping your left hand still, begin loosely twisting them from the top as you slide your hand down to their opposite ends.

3 :: Keeping both sides clamped together in your fists, put the "rope" of necklaces around your neck and fasten each clasp to its corresponding side, while all strands in front remain twisted. (This can be trickier than it sounds; you might want to attach a rubber band around the ends to hold everything together while fastening. Carefully snip off the rubber band when you're done.)

4 :: Slide the piece, as one unit, around your neck until the clasps are in back.

Variation: Link together the clasps of your favorite necklaces from end to end to create an extravagant, layered wraparound necklace.

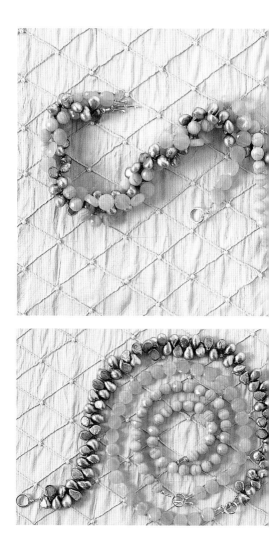

PART THREE

FINISHING TOUCHES

garage sale necklace

So you've tackled every project in the book! Now you are covered in your magnificent new jewelry and already dreaming up a few more of your own designs. You probably have lots of leftover goodies rattling around. Before you begin building a studio addition to your house to hold all of your extras, why not finish up by using them in a fun, mixed necklace? Get out all your odds and ends and start stringing!

HOW TO

By now you're surely a pro. Use your newfound skills to mix up all your extra beads and stones in random order, or create a funky rainbow effect by stringing your beads according to color, like the one shown. Use a big, chunky stone as a pendant and attach with a simple wire-wrapped loop. Add the clasp, and…oh, how you sparkle!

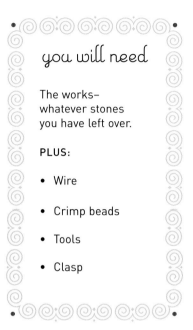

you will need

The works—whatever stones you have left over.

PLUS:

- Wire
- Crimp beads
- Tools
- Clasp

resources

Consult your phone book for local retailers, or check out these online suppliers. Craft stores often stock less expensive beads, which are great for beginners as well as experienced jewelry designers.

www.earthstone.com
Oodles of beads, gems, findings, and miscellaneous jewelry-making materials.

www.firemountaingems.com
An even larger selection of beads, gems, findings, and miscellaneous jewelry-making materials.

www.EasternFindings.com
Great clasps, findings, and all the other essentials.

www.metalliferous.com
A fantastic source for metal parts, wire, and findings.

www.mjtrim.com
The ultimate ribbon and trimming supplier.

www.ebay.com
You never know what treasures you'll find by searching eBay's colossal jewelry section. This is a great place to find pretty vintage jewelry boxes in which to store your growing collection! They also list strands of gemstones for sale, but be wary—it's difficult to verify authenticity until you have them in your hot little hands.

www.intergem.net
Explore local bead and gem tradeshows that visit your area. Start by searching for Web sites that promote them, like this one.

Bead and Button magazine and *Lapidary Journal* can provide you with even more resources, project ideas, and insider design tips.

www.femmegems.com
Designer and design-your-own jewelry.
See you there!